DATA-DRIVEN BUSINESS

TIM PHILLIPS

DATA-DRIVEN BUSINESS

USE REAL-LIFE NUMBERS TO IMPROVE YOUR BUSINESS BY 352%

infiniteideas

The right of Tim Phillips to be identified as the author of this book has been asserted in accordance with the Copyright, Designs and Patents Act 1988.

First published in 2016 by

Infinite Ideas Limited
36 St Giles
Oxford
OX1 3LD
United Kingdom

www.infideas.com

A CIP catalogue record for this book is available from the British Library

ISBN 978–1–908984–60–9

Printed in Britain by 4edge Limited

CONTENTS

INTRODUCTION

Why data? Why 352%? Because Google's 2000 revenue in its first full year of business was $19.1 million. In 2001, its second full year, this jumped to $86.4 million. If Google, which is in the business of data, can grow by 352%, so can you – if you know how to use the data you have, and the data you can generate.

Well, 352% is probably ambitious, at least to begin with. The point is that it is now practical for non-specialists to use basic data and statistics to find out far more about their business, their markets and their customers than was possible only a few years ago. Google has made this the foundation of its business. It is constantly analysing what it does, tweaking it, running experiments, testing products – and, most importantly, learning from what the data tells it.

Google has advantages. Its business is mostly data. It employs many of the biggest brains on the planet. And, if you work for Google, you never have to wait long for tech support to arrive if you get into a mess.

But we can all do more. We can recognize the limitations of what intuition is telling us. We can find out more about our businesses today, and better analyse the potential risks and re-wards of our decisions. We can resolve the nagging questions that no one seems to have an answer to. We can learn to be sceptical about the numbers others use, and so avoid simple mistakes. We can become better managers, and still get home in time to see the kids before they go to sleep.

How do I use this book?

It depends on what you want. Here are a few ideas.

'I'm useless at maths. It's genetic.'

You probably opened this book with a sadness in your heart. You have spent your adult life avoiding numbers, and you tell people that you're one of those people who doesn't have the maths gene. Good news: your genetic makeup will not stop you understanding anything in this book. Miles Kimball and Noah Smith, two academic economists, pointed out in a 2013 article for *Quartz* that even talking about a maths gene sorts people who are learning about numbers into two groups, be-cause kids who struggle at first assume they're genetically no good, and so don't try as hard. The top students relish their supposed genetic advantage, and apply themselves more. But, get this: there is no scientific study that has ever found a maths gene. The effect is purely a social one, based on early experiences and the suitability of your education. You can un-derstand everything in this book. Take it slow. Breathe.

'Work is getting to be all about spreadsheets and charts and I hate it.'

It is. This is true. You're suddenly working with a bunch of people who seem to get it, and you're constantly staring at things and wondering what they mean. Concentrate on our section on the basics: that's 90% (that's a guess) of what you need to do. Keep the book around in case of emergencies.

'We're hopeless at making decisions.'

Good for you: one of the reasons that bad decisions are made, or good decisions aren't made, is a lack of hard information. The most important information is to know where you are now (Part 3), but being able to use data for forecasting (Part 4) is also fundamental. And, of course, better decision-making needs to be built into the way you manage, so Part 5 is all about that.

'My presentations suck.'

You're not alone. Understanding data creates clarity and better storytelling. Parts 2, 5 and 6 are for you.

'I don't trust numbers.'

The comedian Stewart Lee tells a story about a taxi driver who responds dismissively to his arguments by saying sarcastically: 'Oh well, you can prove anything with facts.' In 2013, PR company Edelman asked 31,000 people in 26 countries whether they trusted bosses to tell the truth. Only 18% said they did (it could be worse, it's 13% if you're a politician). This lack of trust is depressing and unnecessary. Let's attack this from both sides. First, become more convincing by using numbers to inform people, and to make decisions (Parts 5 and 6). Second, use Part 7 to learn when people are trying to use data to confuse you.

We've heard a lot about big data in recent years. It promises to revolutionize the way we live and work. But many of us are not even geared up for small data. We continue to use our gut feelings to make decisions, even when they're giving us bad data (find out why your intuition is misleading you in Parts 6 and 7). If you want to grow by 352%, or 35.2%, or 3.52%, and your competitors are using data and you're still stuck on guesswork, your chances are not good (remember, their guess is probably as good as yours already). Businesses that can't make informed decisions are trusting to luck, as are you, if you continue to believe that data is for other people. So there's one more personal reason to read this book: data literacy. In the future, this will be as important as knowing how to read and write. Knowing how to use data well will mean you get to keep your job.

PART 1

LET'S GET DATAFIED

WHAT IS DATAFICATION?

It's an ugly word, but a beautiful idea: when so much of what we do can provide information, we can find out far more that we need to know.

This buzzword is quite new, but the concept is actually several decades old: that's when the geeks of your parents' generation realized that we could capture far more of the world as data if only we knew how. The quest to datafy was frustrated by the problem of measurement: for non-digital systems, something is needed to make them into data. In digital systems, the data was already there.

This is useful: because, as you have been told before, you can't manage what you don't measure. Datafication is a way of building measurement into your work. It's the foundation of what we are going to do in the rest of this book.

To explain: if you wanted to know how much mail your business received 30 years ago, you would have to give someone the long and tedious job of counting it. If you wanted to know how much of that communication was addressed to you, someone would have to extract the mail that was for you from the pile, and count that, every day. And if you wanted to know whether you were getting more mail than your colleagues, someone would have to sort and count for a period of weeks, type out a report, photocopy it and deliver it to you.

Then, if you made a change (for example, delegating a job to a colleague), that poor letter-counter would have to repeat this boring job for weeks, type another report, find the first report in the filing cabinet, put them together with paper clips, maybe try to do some simple statistics... Oh, why bother?

Because you're employing someone to do this work, and that person's time has a cost (at the very least, because counting mail means that person isn't doing something else), a lot of useful data was never collected. Worse, some data would take so long to collect that it would be out of date by the time you had it. It was like steering a boat by looking at the wake behind it.

The world has changed, but many of us (almost all of us) have not kept up. For example, in the UK local government is still rekeying a lot of information, which wastes around two million hours a year, according to a survey by software provider NDL. That's because a lot of data is still transferred on paper, and kept in filing cabinets, or sent from company to company by printing it out and retyping it.

When data is retyped, it introduces errors. And, to save time, we don't retype all of it. So data is effectively lost. Those filing cabinets are dead letter offices. No one will read what's in them.

The UK is actually pretty forward-thinking, so multiply this across the world, in business as well as government, and you can see how much of the world's information will never again be seen. It is lost. You have information like this, and some of it is probably useful. So how do you decide what you need to know, and get hold of the information you need?

- Step 1: Do a data audit. List all your business functions, and the decisions you make. This may be a long and boring process, but you won't need to do it very often. One way to think of it is to list the business functions as problems or challenges that need solutions. Then, list the data that you would ideally need to do those jobs well.

- Step 2: Categorize the data. Some, you will already have, and know where it is. Some you will have, but you don't know where it is. Some you won't have, but you can collect. And finally, there's a bunch of stuff that you don't know and can't get (an example would be your competitor's detailed sales figures).

- Step 3: Prioritize the data you need. Not all data is equal. Some is nice to have; some is fundamental to growing your business. Clearly your priority is to collect data that's important, that you don't have, but can be found. Work your way down the list. You will never get to the bottom of it because your priorities will probably change as you work through it.

- Step 4: Build ways to get that data. Your goal in datafying your business is not to stop yourself from doing the job because you're too busy collecting information on how to do the job. Some of the processes will be easy: for example, installing free analytic software to monitor your webpages, or setting up your security logs. Some will be semi-automated: for example, it might be most efficient to give someone the job of doing a simple weekly report. A simple way to datafy your business is to stop using paper bank statements. Link your accounting software to the on-line feed from your bank, which at the very least will make your VAT return quicker and more accurate.

- Step 5: find a place to put the data. This is often over-looked. Sharing data securely is as important as finding it in the first place. Some organizations fall down on this last step: Harris Interactive reports that 92% of us still share in-formation as email attachments, dramatically increasing the possibility that you will send the wrong document, that you will lose it for evermore in your email in-box, or will ac-cidentally overshare when you leave your phone in a taxi. Better: adopt a secure file-sharing method, like DropBox or Google Drive, or a cloud application to hold your data, so you have a single source of truth.

In the rest of this section we'll have a look at some of the data that's within (relatively) easy reach. Your requirements will vary. But, if you want inspiration, look at the filing cabinet or set of in-trays closest to you, find some numbers, and think: how can I get this digitally?

LEARNING TO COUNT

You can learn a lot just by counting the statistics that your business produces.

There's good news: almost everything we do today counts either activity or results, most of which we routinely ignore. Just by counting, we can immediately make progress.

Counting is a first step to saving money. A simple example: how much do you spend on computer software? Cap Gemini asked CIOs about what they spend, and only 37% thought most of their applications were critical for the business. Three quarters thought that 20% of their apps did the same thing; another 57% thought that a fifth should be retired.

Software tools can describe all the software you use in your business: map this to the money you spend on licenses, and it's not going to be hard to save money (how much you save depends on how aggressive you want to be on consolidation).

Two things about this exercise: the first is that you don't have to be a statistical expert to do this. You simply count what you have, and count what you pay. It might take a few hours to do it, but you'll get those hours back if you have fewer software applications to support. Second, the numbers don't make the decision for you, but are the basis for decision-making: you still have to make trade-offs, you just know what those trade-offs imply.

In this example, you might have three different ways to read email. If you pay three sets of software licences, that's a waste of money. But, if the users dislike changing and have developed shortcuts based on their knowledge of the software (or use mobile apps, for example), then consolidating has a cost too. It's harder to measure, but you can make an attempt to place a value on it. Those values depend on your circumstances, so there's no one correct way to act.

Many of us never check which pages users visit on our websites, although Google Analytics (or some other package you might have) is free. It can show which parts of the site don't get visited, which products people have searched for, or which other sites are sending users to your site. All of these simple counting jobs help, and few take more than an hour to do. Perhaps the problem is that we call this 'analytics', and so it makes it sound harder than counting. It isn't.

When you've done this once, make it someone's job to run the numbers regularly, with reporting synchronized to the decision-making process. For example, every quarter for numbers of visitors to webpages, the day before you have a call with your website developer. Or once a year for software licenses, a month before the big ones come up for renewal.

Accounting data is another rich source of information, but a report compiled by CIMA and Loughborough University found that 45% of SMEs don't use regular management accounts: that is, accounts that count where you spend money, what you make it from, and how that changed from last year. SKS, the company that commissioned the report, points out that 'Without this they will have little more than gut-feel and the bank balance on which to base important decisions.'

SKS has an interest in this: it's in the management accounts business. There are two obvious reasons why small businesses don't prepare these accounts. They might not have time to do it, and/or they can't easily find the data. But even basic cloud accounting software such as Freshbooks or Xero will do this for you, by linking to bank accounts and producing reports automatically. This is the gift of datafication: if you want to know whether you're on target, selling more online than last year, or earning most of your income from just a few products, it has already done the counting for you.

How do you build this into the business? A simple discipline is to schedule a regular meeting based around what you counted, and make it someone's job to make a short presentation each meeting – and make sure the information is right up to date. If you base that meeting around a simple question (such as 'where do we spend most money?' or 'what do people complain about most?'), and keep it short – a few numbers and a quick discussion, with one or two things to do at the end of the meeting, then it needn't be an ordeal.

3

TIME IS MONEY

Measuring how long things take, and how much that time costs, will help (as long as measuring doesn't take too long).

There are some irritations at work that we think about every day, but we never fix them – partly because we don't measure them. There's a company called Atlassian that made an infographic about how we spend our working hours called, encouragingly: 'You waste a lot of time at work'. (See the resources section for a link. Note: there isn't a special category for 'time spent reading infographics'.) Its headline result: 60% or less of the time we spend at work is spent productively. The results were scary enough: 80% of interruptions at work are considered trivial, 47% of respondents considered work to be the biggest time waster at the office, 39% had slept during a meeting.

If you have ever nodded off in a meeting (one of my colleagues once did this in another company's offices. He woke up to hear the person he had travelled to meet saying, 'well, you're obviously very tired...') this research seems like it might tell you something about your life. You might email the infographic to someone in the company, saying, 'we must do something about this', or resolve to change the way you work. But, we all know, that's not going to change anything. You need to datafy the way you allocate time.

Who doesn't want to work shorter hours for the same, or better, result? Why not measure your own productivity, and the productivity of the people around you? If only you had some device to do this. You do, of course, it's called your phone. You have two more devices that would work. They are called a pencil, and paper.

First, record how much time you spend in meetings, in traffic, on calls, writing presentations. A simple app like Toggl can do the basic time recording job: it's like a slightly more sophisticated stopwatch.

Don't do this for a day or a week, because not every day at work is the same, I hope. A month is better. If it's too hard to do using an app, fall back on making a list. Lawyers and accountants have recorded their time this way for hundreds of years, because that's how they bill their clients, so it is possible.

The result: an account of your time, and the time spent by your colleagues. You can use this in three ways:

1. Become a better person. How much time do you spend at work checking Facebook? Would the meeting have been half an hour shorter if you had done 15 minutes of preparation first? If you measure accurately how long it takes to do a job (for example, to write a marketing plan), you can give

people a more accurate forecast of when they can expect to have the work completed.

2. If you're not the boss, when justifying your value to your employer, or arguing that you should be spending less time doing unproductive work, a precise number, with your hourly rate attached to it, can help change minds in a way that a complaint never can. Many of us (the survey at the beginning of the chapter goes into more depth) complain that we spend too much time answering emails or stuck in traffic, because we want to be taken off CC lists or to work from home. This is the data that makes these decisions happen.

3. If you are the boss, this data can help you work out better ways to do things. Warning: this is extremely problematic. If you just tell everyone to log the time they spend doing tasks because you want to save money, clearly everyone is mostly going to be worried about losing their job, or being bullied, even if you don't have this in mind. As a result, they either will refuse to cooperate, or lie. So maybe concentrate on one problem area, or let them work out the problems and solutions among themselves, and report back. Also, note that covert monitoring of staff is against the law in many countries, and is usually rotten management anyway.

I've audited my time, and found it works, as have many of my geeky friends. But I also discovered it works best when you state a goal first. It might be as simple as not working weekends, or deciding which day is best for working from home. When you have a goal in mind, you quickly begin to see the type of improvements you can make, and the trade-offs that will have to be made. For example, one of my geeky friends now has an email signature that tells people he reads his email only at lunchtime and between 5 pm and 6 pm, because when he measured the time he was spending on unproductive message answering, he realized that constant back-and-forth emails were costing his business money. Precise time management made him happier and more productive.

WHAT WOULD TWITTER DO?

A free opinion survey: what could be more valuable?

If you have a business, you are probably also present on social media. You may have a Facebook page, and a Twitter account, and maybe also Google+. Perhaps someone has been sending out pictures of your products on Instagram.

You might also have an email marketing campaign, or a newsletter. You run a blog, which may or may not be updated every week. You spent hours setting up the facility to tweet a blog, so that you can blog your tweets.

Then you count your likes. Social media is all digital: for the first time in history, our attitudes are datafied as soon as we express them. There's so much data, that companies like Facebook and Twitter actually anonymize it, and provide it to data scientists who sell the information. This is called the 'firehose' of social data, for obvious reasons.

You don't need to drink from the firehose. You can count your shares, your retweets and your +1s. Twitter produces analytics on your account, and you use software like Tweetdeck or Sprout Social or SocialOomph to help the analysis. Every time you post, you wait to see who shares it.

These are all good things to do. If people are doing these things (try stopping them – according to Lightspeed GMI, 34.9% of 18–24 year olds in the UK check their social media before even getting out of bed), let's look at what's going on, and how it affects your business. We can be pretty sure that it's better for your company to have 100 likes than one like, and it's great to see something you created being shared, appreciated and passed on. Though, as your blog numbers climb, and your +1s multiply, and you consider taking on a social media manager or putting everyone through a training course, you might also stop to wonder, 'what does this actually mean?'

The short answer is: on its own, not much. These numbers are known as 'vanity metrics'. The more vain you are, the more you value them. But the thing you have counted is a reliable measure only of itself.

Counting your retweets measures precisely the number of people who retweet you. If you use a social media consultant, they might call this your 'share of voice', because that's something a consultant can write on an invoice and get paid for. Retweets or likes do not measure:

- How popular you are

- Whether people will buy something that you Tweeted about

- Whether people like you in real life

People can 'like' you or retweet you for a number of reasons. For example, this MP got a lot of retweets (before he deleted the tweet), and increased his share of voice, but he's probably not enhanced his reputation, his credibility or his number of real-life friends:

To find out more about how social media maps to real life, you can pay for services that will do what is called 'sentiment analysis'. It does this by looking for keywords like 'love'. But, historically, it has been 70% accurate at best – which isn't much better than flipping a coin, and probably not as good as your best existing guess of how much your customers like you. Sentiment isn't easy to measure on a computer: for example, a TV station wants to find out how popular its programme is. Tweeting about hating the programme is negative, but tweeting about hating the bad guy in the same programme is positive, because it shows you're watching/paying attention and motivated to tell the world that you are watching/paying attention. But both tweets may be interpreted as negative sentiment by a computer.

It gets murkier. Even if the sentiment analysis is accurate, it might not mean much in the real world. Tweeting and linking takes a second, few people take it seriously, and you can always delete or unlike afterwards. So it's wrong to always associate social media activity with an intention to spend money or make a serious commitment in real life.

And, finally, the people on social media are much more likely to be young, middle class, educated and from developed countries. So it's easy to rely too much on social data, for these four reasons:

1. A 'like' and an intention to buy are not the same thing

2. People can retweet or 'like' for good and bad reasons

3. There's no evidence that this is a lasting emotion

4. The people who are doing this may not be the people you're interested in

On the other hand, this is a free snapshot that has some useful data in it. It shows what aspect of your company, or your publicity, that people on social media think is interesting. It can show a trend. It can give quick feedback when you make changes or hit problems in one location or with one group. So it's not data about everything, but it's the biggest free thing in datafication ever, and you'd be foolish to ignore it.

5

SIZE DOES MATTER

What is big data, and where can you get some?

If you haven't been hiding out in a place without electricity, you will have noticed people talking about this thing called big data. This is the end-game of datafication: the idea that all the data that the digital world produces might be useful to improve the world that produced it. Or, in our case, help make you 352% more profitable.

Any discussion of big data starts with a statement of how much data there is. Spoiler alert: it's big. Kenneth Cukier and Viktor Mayer-Schönberger, who co-wrote the best book so far on the topic (called, with admirable clarity, *Big Data*) calculated in 2013 that if all the information in the world was copied on to CDs and they were piled up, it would form five separate piles that would all reach the moon.

By now, there would be five more piles, but it doesn't really matter, because you can't make piles that big. The important thing about it is that almost all new information is created digitally. In 2000, about a quarter of all information was digital data. Today, 99% of information is digital.

The promise of big data is that many more things can be known. But it's not that easy. Datafication doesn't guarantee an end result that you can use. Most of the new data is of poor quality or hard to analyse. For example, new CCTV installations are almost all digital these days. But computers can't yet 'watch' your CCTV video and say what they see beyond detecting simple, but important, things like overcrowding. Storing thousands of documents in a word processor format is great if you want to search for a word or phrase, but not so good if you don't have time to read all the documents that searching for that phrase throws up. Most people search because they want to solve a problem, not to provide reading material.

Big data is, by definition, the stuff that's too large and complex for the sort of databases that companies usually run. The capability has to be built using specialist technology, and managed, and updated, and secured. This is difficult and expensive, and out of the reach of most companies. So how can big data benefit you, if you're one of them?

First, the people who use big data are providing all sorts of ways to help you be more efficient, often delivered free. The most obvious example is Google's range of services: think of Google Maps, or personalized Google news feeds in your email, or the reports that Google Analytics generates about your website.

Big data can also solve problems by allowing service providers to build expert systems based on machine learning and artificial intelligence. The simplest is the Amazon 'People who bought this...' recommendation engines. This 'wisdom of crowds' type application has big-data-like properties: it isn't perfect, because all big data does is look for patterns in the data that it has spotted before, and matches them to what it knows of your needs. But it's quick and better than a guess, and as we know, you waste 60% of your time at work, and gut feel is a bad guide to decision-making.

These expert systems are datafying functions that were previously human skills, such as typing and translating. Do you get behind when typing up notes? The quality of dictation software is far better than it used to be, not because we have created new rules for software, but because computers use big data to teach themselves. Expert systems learn by being fed audio of people speaking that's culled from the internet, with the transcript of what they are saying, and letting them learn for themselves. If you don't believe that dictation software is useful because you tried it in the 1990s and it was rubbish (it was), try an online application like Transcribe and be amazed.

These applications are free, or nearly free. They are also about big data behind the scenes: you're just using the output. Can you do more? Yes and no.

There are two ways in which big data may be a good investment for even a small business. The first is that you can use big data science to improve your own data: an example would be external credit checking, or being able to automatically spot bargains when they come up for sale on online auctions. This being the internet, there's an online community of data scientists who can use big data to do this, called Kaggle. Businesses post competitions with prizes, and the geeks compete to get the best results. Recent prizes have been won for better ways to do claims management for BNP Paribas ($30,000) and for discovering which customers of Santander are happiest ($60,000).

You might not have this type of cash. Not many businesses do. For smaller sums you could, for example, do some trend analysis using Facebook data by hiring a market research company. But you're still going to need to pay for the results, so this isn't a quick decision. You need to think carefully first about what sort of insight you want to buy, and how you are going to use it in your business. Research by Insite Consulting shows that about half of research findings never get used to change business decisions. It's literally a waste of money.

You might also decide to work with the data yourself. How hard can it be? Very hard, is the answer. The data is there: the initiative called open data is dedicated to collating big data, and making either it (or the results of their analysis) available to the public. In the UK the Open Data Institute is leading the way, and the UK government is publishing data on all sorts of things, from planned roadworks to obesity statistics. In other countries, national data is increasingly made available for anyone who wants to download it. So there are lots of large sets of data, or data feeds, available. But big data's value is in its analysis.

This is difficult: in the last 20 years, billions of pounds have been wasted by companies getting tied up in data, and finding more questions than answers: in 1998, four out of five of the first wave of big data projects failed, according to analyst Ovum. The dominant reason was that they couldn't be sure whether the insights they generated were useful in creating a better business even if they were true, and so they didn't know whether to invest in projects, and they didn't know whether to make business decisions based on the facts.

So, ironically, you might get the best results from big data by starting small: use free or nearly free services to improve business processes before you make big investments.

PART 2

FIVE DATA BASICS

KEEP YOUR DATA ALIVE

Once you have your data, make sure it lives as numbers, not text.

I was speaking to the head of a newspaper's graphics department, let's call her Carol, about how she managed to make complicated visual data into neat graphs and diagrams. Unwisely, I mentioned PDFs.

'I'd have them made illegal', Carol said, rolling her eyes. 'I can't count the amount of hours I have wasted because people have emailed me a PDF and said [she puts on a silly voice at this point] "can you make a graph out of that please Carol?" NO I CAN'T.'

So! Here we are, with data. How do we keep it? Here's a clue: not in a PDF. Overwhelmingly, we keep the piles of data we will need in two places: in a database and in a spreadsheet. Those files might be on our laptops, on servers or in the cloud somewhere, but what matters is that they remain in a format that you can work with.

Databases are what are used to store large amounts of data. The details of how they do this are far too technical to explain here, so we've all dodged a bullet when I say I'm not going to get into it. You're probably more familiar with how spreadsheets function. If you work with budgets or schedules or any other small-scale data, you've used one – probably Microsoft Excel.

Databases and spreadsheets have something in common: the data is arranged as a table, in rows and columns. We've forgotten what a small piece of genius the spreadsheet is: originally used on paper by accountants, when they were recreated on a computer in 1979 as VisiCalc, they became the first 'killer app' for the PC.

The beauty of a spreadsheet is that the table has two functions. It means you can work first with the data, by making a row that adds up all the other rows, for example. The numbers and names in a spreadsheet are the data. In a PDF or a Word document, the numbers cease to live:

If someone needs to use them, they have to copy them out again, or cut and paste them if they are lucky.

If the numbers are calculated (for example by adding subtotals together), when they reach a PDF or a Word document you're probably going to break that link.

When the source for the data is updated, that update never reaches a word processor document. They begin to get out of date the moment they are created. In a database, and in a spreadsheet if you're a little bit clever, you can make sure your data stays current.

So, having laboured to create beautiful data, please keep it alive. If it's dead, you can make it look good, but it's all show. Just ask Carol (better idea: don't ask her). This is the fundamental rule of business data: you can't run a business on last year's facts.

DRAW A TABLE

Everyone knows how to make a good table out of their data, don't they?

Once you have put your data into the spreadsheet, you need to be able to communicate it. Drawing an effective table is often the most efficient way to communicate data, but it's also one of the most often abused. So, before we get into the long grass, it is worth taking five minutes to work out the difference between a good table and a bad one.

Edward Tufte, an information design specialist, is probably the person who thinks most about how to communicate data effectively. Tufte maintains that 'chart junk', which is the sort of fancy formatting that you get when you click on a formatting button in a spreadsheet package, 'is a clear sign of statistical stupidity; use these designs in a presentation and your audience will rightly conclude that you don't know all that much about statistical data.' You can find discussion on this on his (suitably austere) website, which is listed in the resources.

Tufte's principle for making tables is that every item of data, and every design element, should help us to understand the story. This is harder than it may seem, but the most appropriate way to do it is by removing distractions, and organizing and grouping the information so it matches the way we think.

Cancer site	Relative survival rate, % (SE)			
	5 years	10 years	15 years	20 years
Oral cavity and pharynx	56.7 (1.3)	44.2 (1.4)	37.5 (1.6)	33.0 (1.8)
Oesephagus	14.2 (1.4)	7.9 (1.6)	7.7 (1.6)	5.4 (2.0)
Stomach	23.8 (1.3)	19.4 (1.4)	19.0 (1.7)	14.9 (1.9)
Colon	61.7 (0.8)	55.4 (1.0)	53.9 (1.2)	52.3 (1.6)
Rectum	62.6 (1.2)	55.2 (1.4)	51.8 (1.8)	49.2 (2.3)
Liver and intrahepatic bile duct	7.5 (1.1)	5.8 (1.2)	6.3 (1.5)	7.6 (2.0)
⋮	⋮	⋮	⋮	⋮
Leukaemias	42.5 (1.2)	32.4 (1.3)	29.7 (1.5)	26.2 (1.7)

Table: Most recent period estimates of relative survival rates, by cancer site

An example is a table of cancer survival rates, as reported by Hermann Brenner in the paper 'Long-term survival rates of cancer patients achieved by the end of the 20th century: a period analysis', (Lancet, number 360, October 12, 2002, pages 1131–1135), which was widely referenced in newspapers when it was published. The original table looked like the one above.

It's far from the being the worst table, but it's hard for a non-specialist to work out what it means, or where the good news is, which cancers are most serious, or where most progress has been made – which is what we all want to know. Tufte's simplification of the table (which contains all the same data) looks like the one shown opposite:

Estimates of relative survival rates, by cancer site

% survival rates and their standard errors

	5 year		10 year		15 year		20 year	
Prostate	98.8	0.4	95.2	0.9	87.1	1.7	81.1	3.0
Thyroid	96.0	0.8	95.8	1.2	94.0	1.6	95.4	2.1
Testis	94.7	1.1	94.0	1.3	91.1	1.8	88.2	2.3
Melanomas	89.0	0.8	86.7	1.1	83.5	1.5	82.8	1.9
Breast	86.4	0.4	78.3	0.6	71.3	0.7	65.0	1.0
⋮	⋮		⋮		⋮		⋮	

I've missed off the bottom of the table, because you can understand the design as soon as you look at it. Why is it so much clearer? Here are some suggestions for making a good table:

Order the information so the most important is at the top. Tufte's table has the cancer with the best survival rate after five years at the top. Why? Because, if you are diagnosed, you want to know what your chances are compared to other cancers. It's how we think, and it's how we make decisions.

Don't use jargon in the column and row headings. Some will know what a standard error is (it's a measure of showing how 'spread out' the data is), but '% (SE)' is hard to understand. But note how the legend – placed at the top where you will read it before you read the numbers – explains what the numbers mean.

Use as few lines as possible, but no less. There are eight statistics for each cancer, but four columns. Grouping the mean and the standard error together, without lots of lines and boxes, draws the eye to the most important information. There are no brackets around the standard errors any more, which makes them easier to read.

Don't simply apply the formats suggested by Excel. Most of them are too fussy. Look at Tufte's table: there is almost no formatting, because lines and colours distract from the numbers.

In business, data is used to make decisions. It's how we're going to get that 352% improvement I promised you: by making different decisions. So a good spreadsheet table is the single most important asset you have when precision is important. As with this example, it might be all you need to find the important information to reach a conclusion. But also, the data is live: unlike with a PDF, you can use it to do the next thing, which is to make a graph.

8

DRAW A GRAPH

Graphs can obscure information as well as describe it.

Open Excel, type in data, highlight data, click on a chart type, select chart, copy, paste into PowerPoint, present. We've all done it, and then been able to look at the sad faces of the people we're presenting to as they struggle to grasp your important point.

Here are three ways (not the only three) to make your charts more understandable. Your rule of thumb: you should be able to put up a chart in a presentation, say 'see what I mean?' and everyone should be able to work it out for themselves.

Make the axes the right length

Look at the chart of the growth of stuff overleaf:

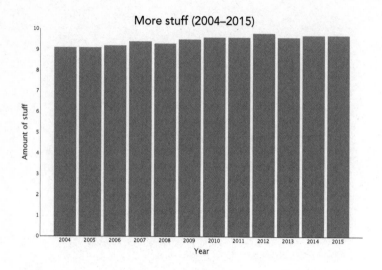

The title tells you that there's more stuff, but you have to squint to see that there is. In fact, a better title for the graph as it is presented is that the amount of stuff is more or less the same every year.

The question: do you start with the axis at zero or not? (The problem of truncated vertical axes was first raised in 1954 in *How to lie with statistics* by Darrell Huff, still the most popular book on statistics ever written) If there's a roughly equal possibility of zero stuff and 10 stuff, you should start at zero – the important information will be that the amount has been more than 9 for 12 years! Well done. But, if possible amounts of stuff will probably never be less than 9, emphasize the story you want to tell, not the nine-tenths that you don't. On the next page you can see the same graph, with the presentation now matching the title.

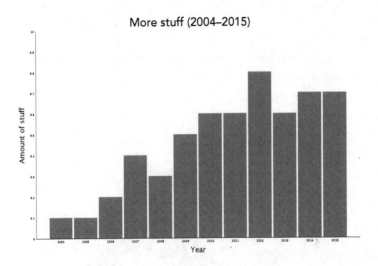

More stuff (2004–2015)

Beware of 3D

The beauty of a flat oblong bar chart is that it shows one thing: the length of the bar matches the data. It's impossible to ignore. But Excel (other spreadsheets are available) offers 3D shapes, in case we need to be entertained rather than informed. At best, the extra dimension doesn't offer new information, while distracting us from the height of the bar.

At worst, it gives us the wrong information. Excel offer graphs made of 3D cone shapes. We should be looking at the height of the cone, but our brains tend to overestimate the difference.

The worst sin is to use a 3D shape. Look at the graphic overleaf.

The second moneybag is twice the height of the first one. But, in our minds, we also imagine that it is twice as deep and see that it is twice as wide. The volume of the second bag is eight times to volume of the first one. This is always used to exaggerate differences. There are no clip art police, so you can do this if you want. But you're faking what the data tells you, not using it. At least, if you know about it, you'll be ready for anyone who tries it on you.

Our revenues have doubled!

In this case, if you're really sold on moneybag clip art, the correct way to do it is to use twice as many identically-sized moneybags for the second number, and lay them out side-by-side so the length of the line of moneybags can be compared. It's like a bar, but made up of little bags.

Too much pie

Pie charts are everywhere in presentations, because tables are seen as rather old hat. But often the pie chart is just a picture, with little information that we can use. Opposite is an example; it has a legend and everything, but which slice is biggest? In tests, most people would say the one at the front, because it's closest so we see it as larger. But even a 2D pie chart would make it hard to distinguish these three similar-sized slices.

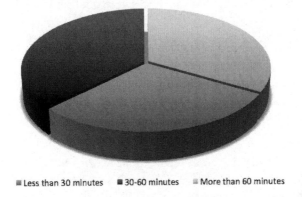

■ Less than 30 minutes   ■ 30-60 minutes   ▨ More than 60 minutes

You could put the numbers on the pie slices, or percentages. That's better, but it often takes a lot of reading to find the story – especially if the slices aren't in an obvious big-to-small order.

Show your pie charts to someone, and ask them to quickly tell you what they say. If they can't tell you in 10 seconds, you probably need a bar chart instead:

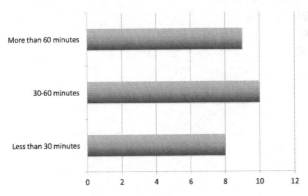

Based on 27 people in Manchester office, January 2016

This is an ugly-ass bar chart because it has shaded bars, like they're little tubes. Why? Because that's what Excel gave me as a default. Complain to Microsoft. But at least we can now see that the middle bar is the largest, and after a few seconds we can read how many are in each category using the vertical lines. That's an improvement. It would have been better maybe to have a little row of person shapes instead of each bar, and then it would remind us that the numbers are people. But that takes longer to do, and Excel doesn't do it automatically, though it should by now.

I have a radical suggestion for you here. If you have simple data – say five numbers or fewer – and you want to report them, why not just leave it as a table, like before? This has all the information of the previous two charts, it's quicker to read, and the data is impossible to misinterpret:

How long is your commute?

It takes me ...	How many of us?
Less than 30 minutes	8
30–60 minutes	10
More than 60 minutes	9

Based on 27 people in Manchester office, January 2016

FIND A TREND

Graphs often tell a story about the relationships in data. Identifying this story helps you make better decisions.

Graphs don't prove a relationship, as we will see later, but they definitely suggest one and, for many purposes, that's a good start. On the next page is a table listing how often the British government described rich people as 'wealth creators', year by year.

I make no comment on whether people who have more money create wealth (by starting companies and giving jobs to people, and buying big houses on which other people earn commission) or consume wealth (if they use it to buy a second house that stands empty, someone else could have used that wealth to buy a house and live in it). It's a subjective judgement, and different types of politician have different points of view.

Year	Mentions per 100,000 articles
2000	46.7
2001	36.9
2002	40.8
2003	33.6
2004	41.2
2005	49.2
2006	40.3
2007	78.5
2008	83.9
2009	129.4
2010	127.9
2011	152.5
2012	201.7

You can see the number goes up, but not much more. So now we can do the basic scatter plot, as shown opposite.

This is interesting: now you can see the numbers go up. We read left to right, and reading a graph like this suggests a story in our mind. It seems we have a trend.

This is the first time in this book we have had to think hard about the problem of interpretation. The dots are statistics: a statistic represents information but is not the information itself. In this case they're measurements of article frequency in a database called Factiva.com, which collects articles from the world's newspapers and magazines. But statistics are usually measured with error (the database might not be complete) and trends in real life aren't neat, like school science experiments. There are lots of influences on this data. So the story I tell is just one of many possible stories.

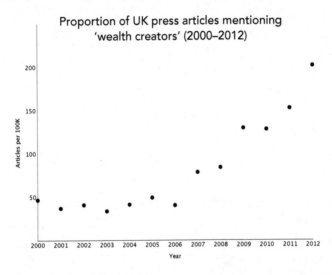

Proportion of UK press articles mentioning 'wealth creators' (2000–2012)

What's the story? We're on pretty solid ground to point out that there's a trend: politicians used the term increasingly during the period shown in the graph. Note: if I had just measured the first and last year, and the last year was higher, that's not a trend, it's a difference.

So, maybe we could join up the dots to make the trend more obvious, like the graph overleaf.

It's more interesting visually, but we could do better. No one would suggest that the number of articles moved as precisely as this. Our higgledy-piggledy line has made the graph clearer, but not the story. It would be better if we could draw a straight line that represented a trend.

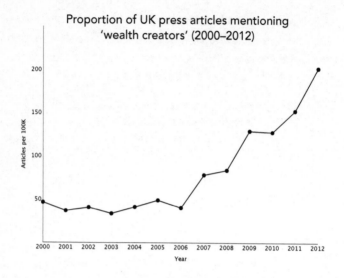

Proportion of UK press articles mentioning 'wealth creators' (2000–2012)

To draw the line, statisticians overwhelmingly use a method called 'least squares approximation'. This takes all the scattered dots and calculates a line that minimizes the square of the distance from each dot to that line. We call this the line of best fit: don't worry if you're not a statistician, you can find a function to draw it in your spreadsheet's graphing function. But, here a single line might not be very informative: we can see that the dots don't seem to go in a straight line. So a straight line of best fit would have most dots above it at the beginning and end of our plot, and most below in the middle. This is not a very good story.

Have a look at the graph on the next page though. I divided the data into two parts. From 2000 to 2006, the best fit line was flat. From 2006 to 2012, it zoomed up. It seems, from this, that the term 'wealth creators' became popular after 2006.

Is this the truth? The statistics are accurate, but trend analysis is always subjective. A simple bar chart would also tell the story that the frequency of mentions was going up, and maybe that's all we need to know. We can speculate that someone made a decision to use it at about that time, but that's all it is: informed speculation.

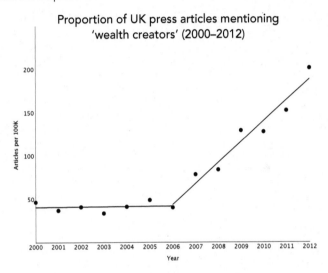

Proportion of UK press articles mentioning 'wealth creators' (2000–2012)

The point though is that just putting numbers in a table, or points on a chart isn't a way to make better decisions. Trends are important. They either suggest that we should find out what's going on if we don't know what caused the trend, or that something may be having an effect, if we have some idea. The longer the trend and the closer the dots to the line, the more it suggests that there's something to find out.

10

FIND AN AVERAGE

Averaging can make information clearer, but there's more than one average – picking the wrong one can hide what you really need to know.

In 1918 John Mecklin coined a phrase that has been tossed around regularly by statisticians ever since, when he published a paper called 'The Tyranny of the Average Man' in the *International Journal of Ethics*.

What is this so-called tyranny? Mecklin can explain. 'Capri's romantic spell suffices even without the aid of Tacitus' biting phrases to remind the traveller of the…', hang on, it's not that bit. 'Our modern tyrant is hydra-headed, myriad handed, and…', oh, do get on with it. Eventually he tells us that he objects to 'the tawdry and commonplace sentimentality of the cheap novel, the impossible wit of the pink Sunday supplement, the utterly inane songs of the popular vaudeville.'

Mecklin's objection, snootily expressed, is the entirely reasonable one that we pay far too much attention to the taste of the majority, and give too little regard to the exceptional. Sitting in the University of Pittsburgh, watching the birth of mass socialism and the spread of democracy from afar, he is both fascinated and threatened by the habits of ordinary people, which he complained would dominate decision-making.

At this point, we must note that his essay is made entirely from the contents of his own head: he doesn't give any examples of 'average' taste, or show how much it is different from the tastes of the rich and successful people he so admired, or provide evidence that what the majority desired was objectively worse than any other choice.

And, of course, it's simply not true in every case. We live in a world where both Adele and Rage Against The Machine can sell CDs, and people can play football or 3D chess for fun. But, for our needs, he does have one useful point. The average often distracts us, and obscures more useful information.

There are three commonly-used averages, all of which are useful:

1. The mean. This is what most people would think of as the average. We add up every statistic and divide it by the number of data points. The mean of 1, 3, 3, 4, 4, 6 is 21/6, or 3.5. If we want to know about the birth rate, for example, the mean is the most sensible statistic: in the UK in 1964, the World Bank recorded 18.8 live births per 1,000 people in the UK. In 2013, the number was 12.2. Interesting.

2. The median. The problem with the mean is that outliers – very high or very low numbers – can have a distorting

effect. So, if you have customers that buy 1, 3, 3, 4, 4, 6 and 28, the mean average customer spends 49/7, or 7. But six out of the seven customers spent less than that, so it's a poor guide for decision-making: your 'typical' customer doesn't spend 7. The median is the middle number when you list them in order – in this case, the fourth out of seven, which is 4, and it's a better average when there are a few weird high numbers.

3. The mode. This is the number you see most often. It's what the largest group does (or is), and so it's good for setting priority. If the mean average number of items that people visiting your web site buy is 7, but 8 visitors out of 10 buy nothing at all, then the mode average purchase is zero, and that might be a good place to start if you want to make changes.

But, the average might obscure information. If you're a supermarket or a government, you're often interested in the whole population as an average. If you are a holiday company for example, you're more often interested in separating the data into different segments before doing any averaging. The mean number of births per woman is declining, but it's often more useful to know about the different groups that make up the average. For a holiday company it might be more useful to know that, for women born since 1981, the median and mode number of births at age 30 is zero: half of them hadn't started a family in their thirties, according to the UK Office of National Statistics. This affects the number of each type of holiday you offer.

An average is also flawed if you want to identify what will happen, rather than what just happened. In any industry there are segments that are what statisticians call 'leading indicators', and we might call 'trendsetters'. Think of fashion: by the time the average that you measure changes, it's too late. You want to identify the 100 people that the mass market tends to copy, and research their data so that you can make better predictions.

A good example is your customer satisfaction data. The average customer score might not change much, but that's made up of a small number of very satisfied customers (who might be the best ones to market to) and a group of very unhappy customers (who might leave), and the rest (who probably don't care much either way).

Treating every customer as the average might be disappointing for your fans, too little too late for potential defectors, and irrelevant for the rest. A real-life example: when UK telecoms company O2 broke apart the mean average of its customer satisfaction rating, and added up the positive contribution of making satisfied customers happier and the negative risk of ignoring unsatisfied customers, it found that helping unhappy customers had more effect on its profitability than distributing rewards equally, or rewarding its fans. In marketing jargon, we call this segmentation, and you'll also be confronted with segments based on gender, age, spending power or habits (with names such as 'experienced moms' or 'individual urban trend'), rather than polices based on the mean, median or mode.

Defeat the tyranny of averages by asking what the average really means: does it help you make a decision? Averages of the whole population are helpful, but remember that data you can act on usually involves looking into what makes up that average.

PART 3

WHERE ARE YOU NOW?

11

WHAT DOES THAT FLASHING LIGHT MEAN?

Data dashboards often seem great for a day or two, then we learn to ignore them. But a good dashboard is a powerful data-driven decision tool.

Acting on data means being able to find the data when you need it. Many businesses use a dashboard, either formal or informal, to put all the information together. But creating a good dashboard isn't as easy as dropping all your business data on a screen.

Your dashboard is a living report of what's going on in the business, and they can be powerful tools for decision-makers, not least because they create good data habits. If your dashboard is working as it should, when anyone asks a question, your first thought is: let's see what the dashboard says about that. Counterintuitively though, the biggest failure in dashboards is that they do too much. If the dashboard is badly designed, the next thought is: I'm not sure what this information means.

The elements of a good dashboard are that:

- It gathers the information you need to do your job on one screen

- It updates it regularly, so you know you have the information that you need

- It suggests what is important

Increasingly you can find dashboards on the front screen of the applications you use. For example, accountancy software will give you a quick summary of information when you log in. But too often we skip this screen, or never bother to use it properly.

So, whether you use an external developer to create a custom dashboard for you, or you set up a piece of commercial software, it must be done properly. Sadly, this is rarely the case. So let's look as some common dashboard fails, and how to avoid them.

The firehose

It's tempting to make a dashboard using every piece of information you can dredge up. So your cash-flow sits next to latest tweets, below news headlines, alongside the customer satisfaction score. You need to be able to read the dashboard, so stick to a few important measures that are grouped logically. In an accountancy dashboard, for example, place the outstanding debtors above the list of overdue invoices to chase.

Is that data good or bad?

Every reported statistic should give some idea of whether it's getting better or worse, whether it is ahead or behind target. Your eye should be drawn to numbers that need action. In a workflow or a spreadsheet, for example, use conditional formatting to colour 'problem' cells red, so you don't have to look for them. This implies that, before you build a dashboard, you have to set your targets.

Fancy formats

There's a commercial design idea that the dashboard must look like the cockpit of an aeroplane or a racing car. The design of those dashboards is carefully done, but they are designed for experts. Also, simple bar charts or trend lines are easier to understand and more accurate than 3D pie charts or fake speed gauges, which often aren't used to report the rate of something, just the amount of it.

Is it fresh?

Your dashboard should automatically update your data for you. You can't make good decisions with out-of-date information. If you're setting up an application, then take time to configure automatic bank feeds or news feeds (and, if you can't get them, you should switch to an application that can). This is irritating and fiddly at first, but it pays off every day.

What do I do?

Just as many of us learn to tolerate an inbox with 3,000 unread emails, we quickly learn to ignore a dashboard that has a flashing light or a red bar on the graph if we don't immediately know what we're meant to do about it. This causes inertia. If it's information about a process you can't affect or isn't relevant, why is it on your dashboard? If you're not sure how urgent it is, think about reporting a number, not just a flashing light (90% of target is different to 50%), or have an amber light as well as green and red, or a system of one to five stars. Finally, you might not know why there's a problem, in which case you should be able to click through to the underlying data.

The first step, then, is to look for dashboards in your everyday applications. For example, if you are a small business your accounting software will usually offer you a snapshot view when you log in. If social media is your thing, any social media manager can be configured to open with a report screen. Every time you see one of them, take 15 minutes to configure it, and set it as a home screen for that application. It's a bit tedious at first, but it gets you thinking about what information you need, and which is just distracting. An example: the average length of time that every customer takes to pay isn't as useful as a list of invoices that are more than 60 days old. Revisit your dashboard regularly, and take out redundant information.

If you want to custom-design a dashboard for your business's key performance indicators, then there are several commercial companies that can help. Many use a free trial to hook you in, but remember that you and your colleagues will simply ignore a poorly designed dashboard. Also remember that your applications must be able to produce timely KPI data feeds for the dashboard. Coordinating this is usually the longest and hardest part of the project.

Finally, you might want to employ a software developer. In which case, find one that has experience in interface design, the more logical and less flash the better.

TRACK YOUR CHANGES

Many companies run a tracker survey. But, like the numbers they report, not all trackers are equal.

You don't know where you're going to end up if you don't know where you are today, and in which direction you are travelling. This applies to what customers, suppliers or staff think of you, just as much as how many widgets you sold yesterday. A continuous customer survey is the rationale for the research tool known as a 'tracker'. The idea is to sample the same basic data over and over again, at regular time intervals, so that you can follow a trend by giving it a simple score.

The most important thing is not how often you ask, it's the questions. A tracker must record answers to the same question(s), asked in the same way, of roughly the same people. The output will result in a number. This statistic goes up if business is good, and down if bad. Most companies with a tracker put it on their dashboards.

That's easy. But that's also where the easy bit stops. Many companies have useless or inaccurate trackers, that stagger on like data-driven zombies long after staff have learned to ignore them. 'The measures that businesses are currently tracking are not necessarily the right ones', warns Phil Codling, research and insight manager at the Institute of Customer Service.

'Today's tracking surveys ask the wrong questions, and they ask far too many of them', is the conclusion of 'The Trouble with Tracking', a white paper written by Jan Hofmeyr, who created the conversion model tracking system. Only ask a question that's relevant to how you're going to make a decision, and which implies an action if the tracker goes down (or up). Companies ask too many questions on their tracker survey because 'survey creep' is natural: people like more information. The trouble is that respondents don't bother to fill in long surveys every month, or just make up the answers. So you get bad information – your trackers bob up and down randomly.

A good tracker, counterintuitively, doesn't move much, because it is responding to strategic trends rather than what happened the day before. This is about long-term benefits, not short-term fixes.

The most often-used tracker at the moment is the one known as Net Promoter Score (NPS). It was developed in 2003 by management consultants Bain. Consultants discovered that the answer to the question: 'how likely are you to recommend (our product / service / company) to friends or family?' on a scale of 0 to 10, was a good indicator of future growth.

The score is made by taking the numbers of promoters (scores of 9 or 10) and subtracting the number of detractors (6 and below). Companies use it to track their customer service, to prioritize projects (those generating the best NPS drive fastest company growth) or to compare offices or departments.

It's controversial, of course, as are all trackers. For example, the tracker has to be there to drive decisions, not just as a reporting tool, so its ups and downs have to be discussed. Many businesses don't trust their trackers as a source of decision-making data, in which case they are literally a waste of money.

Also, a tracker is an indicator that something is wrong or right, but doesn't immediately tell you what that is. So it is an early warning and a quick feedback tool, but it doesn't run the business. You have to do that. It will, however, tell you if you're heading in the right direction in a succinct way.

On the other end of the scale, organizations that obsess on their trackers, for example tying them to too-large bonus payments, can sometimes become businesses in which people try to manipulate the number on the tracker rather than to improve profitability – for example by trying to boost the scores of the people who are neither promoter or detractor, whether or not that has an effect on sales.

So what big questions should a tracker be used for? I asked Rob Markey at Bain, who created NPS. He suggests three categories:

1. Competitive benchmarking. Is your tracker score higher than the score that your competitor gets? This, Bain has found, is correlated with your growth rate.

2. Customer relationships. What do the people who buy from you think? This is useful for spotting problems with marketing or customer service before they become serious.

3. Experience-triggered measures. You can do this by surveying customers on their experience immediately when they buy from you or open an account. You can use this to fix bad processes or improve communication.

But, whatever you use it for, a tracker has to be simple enough, and shared widely enough, and incentivized, so that people who can change it know and care about the number. In this way, moving the tracker becomes the decision-making process. If people know what they should be doing, and the number shows whether they are being successful, the simplicity of the tracker statistic can become the most powerful piece of data in your business.

ERRORS ADD UP

Many numbers are reported precisely, but that doesn't mean they are accurate.

People routinely ask 'exactly what are the numbers?' but it's impossible to be both fast and accurate. Knowing where you are today involves being comfortable with a level of temporary vagueness, because something is better than nothing at all. It's impossible to ever really know the all the data you need.

We don't even know how much stuff our home country produces to within a few billion either way. But we still use suspiciously precise numbers to make policies and write newspaper articles on how well the economy is doing.

Every quarter, every country estimates the sum of the value of all the goods it produces, known as its Gross Domestic Product, or GDP. The level of GDP and GDP growth is one of the most important numbers possible: it influences the policy of governments and central banks. It helps businesses decide whether and where to invest. It tells us whether we're in a boom or a recession, and gives us the first report of changes in the economy.

Like the official statistics on unemployment, credit or investment, the announcement of the quarterly GDP figures is keenly awaited. The only problem is, the figure that is announced will be wrong.

We know it's wrong because all official figures are later revised. For GDP, the figures are revised the next quarter, the next year, and so on. When the OECD, an economic think tank that measures the world's developed countries, analysed recent GDP announcements, it discovered that, on average, three years afterwards, the average correction across all countries was 0.2 percentage points. Sounds insignificant? That represents an average measurement error of $200 billion.

This isn't because government statisticians are bad at their jobs. GDP, like unemployment or job creation or your company's annual turnover, is a measure that is constructed from many other figures, which are all measured separately. Each one of those numbers is measured with an error, and the errors add up.

It's important to be as accurate as possible, but reporting statistics isn't just about getting the right number. Time is also a factor: we need a rough idea of where we are today. If we waited three years to report GDP, then governments and businesses wouldn't be able to make decisions. There's a trade-off.

Similarly, you need the best knowledge that you can get at the right time. It's not possible to measure without error, so you need to decide the value of waiting until you have better data, or of putting in more time to do a more accurate calculation. Often a simple, rough calculation is good enough, as long as everyone knows what the margin of error is.

So there are two problems, one if you're doing the reporting, and one if you're using the numbers to make a decision. So we tend to overestimate the reliability of what we measure, and we also tend to attribute trends or patterns to data when we might just be looking at measurement error.

A simple discipline: when you make a table or a graph, don't overstate the precision of the figures. Often we do this because Excel tells us to do it, by calculating exact percentages. So you do an internal survey of your colleagues to work out where to hold the Christmas party, and get 23 responses:

In the office	4
At a restaurant	13
In a nightclub	6

My spreadsheet told me that this means:

Location	Percentage
In the office	17.39%
At a restaurant	56.52%
In a nightclub	26.09%

But what do the decimal places mean? 17%, 57% and 26% would be fine. Though 4, 13 and 6 tell you everything you need to know, which is that most people want to go to a restaurant.

These figures are counted, but measured figures should also be reported with caution. Your weight varies during the day; so don't worry too much if you are 0.5kg heavier after dinner tonight than you were yesterday morning. That may be a change, but it may be measurement error. The average of many measurements may be better – but, again, don't overdo the precision.

When you're reading survey results, ask the questions from the other end. Reported statistics should always give an idea of the potential impact of measurement error. Good tables and graphs will show measurement error for a degree of confidence (90% or 95% are most common). An error of plus or minus 2% with 90% confidence means that, if you measure 100 times, 90 times the data would be within 2% each way of the recorded level.

This is extremely important to know if you are using the statistics to make decisions. If you use a company to supply figures to you, ask them to draw these intervals as 'error bars':

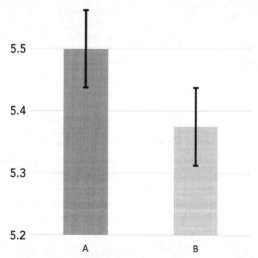

It looks like the right hand column is smaller than the one on the left, but the error bars overlap: we can't be sure if this means the underlying statistic we are measuring is different in the two populations, given our confidence interval (if the error bars don't overlap, then we can be sure).

An example: recently I was presented with a survey that showed the level of worry that CEOs had about security, on a scale of 1 to 10. The company that did the survey was delighted because the service they sold solved a problem that rated top for priority, scoring 6.9. But the scores for other problems were between 6.8 and 6.5, so I asked the people who did the survey how big the error bars were. The company had asked only a small number of CEOs, and their answers varied a lot, which meant that really all we could say is that CEOs were more or less equally worried about many problems – if the researchers had done the survey again with another group of similar CEOs, the priority order would likely be different.

This negative result is actually useful information: it shows that CEOs haven't prioritized one threat, so they probably would be more receptive to information and education rather than a sales pitch for a specific thing. But, if you overestimate accuracy because the numbers are more precise than they should be, you'd never work that out.

PART 4

WHERE ARE YOU GOING?

14

FORWARD GUIDANCE

You don't know the future, but it's helpful to have a go at predicting it anyway.

We may think we promote people who achieve the most but the statistics show we often select people who are overconfident in their opinions, mistaking this for expertise. Daniel Kahneman, who won the Nobel prize in 2002 for his work on how people make (imperfect) decisions, warns that 'Experts don't know exactly where the boundaries of their expertise are... We associate leadership with decisiveness. That perception of leadership pushes people to make decisions fairly quickly... We deeply want to be led by people who know what they're doing and who don't have to think about it too much.'

We seem to favour chancers who get lucky. As Kahneman says, 'Some achieve a reputation for great successes when in fact all they have done is take chances that reasonable people wouldn't take.' Or, as the management guru Tom Peters says:

'Good managers have a bias for action.'

Is this a problem? Yes, because the bias for action has a cost: it also means a bias against analysis. We are more inclined to trust an overconfident leader, less inclined to question, and therefore rely less on what we could observe or learn when we forecast the future.

There is, of course a problem with the future. It hasn't happened yet, so we are always guessing. Forecasting is an increasingly important part of business, because the investments needed to take advantage of a change in conditions are more effective if they anticipate events than if they follow them. The trackers and dashboards are fine, but they don't tell you what to do next.

The data deficit in forecasting encourages the bias for action, with all the downsides that Kahneman worries about. But how do we forecast better?

The first point is that you can't forecast perfectly. There will always be errors. As the economist Paul Samuelson said in 1966: 'The stock market has forecast nine of the last five recessions.'

The second is that there are many ways to do forecasting:

Trend analysis, using past performance to predict the future, is practical, you can do it, but it has the flaw that it assumes the underlying situation stays the same. The most important future guidance is often the prediction that something is about to change. Trend analysis is weakest in this area.

Predictive analytics (the big data of forecasts) using complex mathematical models, is powerful but needs investment (and lots of data).

Taking a consensus of experts – rather like the panels of financial analysts that decide whether to buy, sell or hold a stock, intuitively pools their knowledge, but has the flaw that all the experts see the same data, and so there is a tendency to groupthink.

Prediction markets are fascinating, but rare. If your internal staff all could place a bet on whether something would happen and when, or how much it would be worth, what would they bet on, and how much? The prediction market, like a bookmaker's odds, combines these bets. Prediction markets for elections, for example, often beat expert consensus because those who know little bet small amounts. Futures markets (and, to a limited extent, the stock market) are prediction markets.

There is, however, a value to having a strong forecasting team above simply getting the right answer more often. It allows you to set a direction for the business. Central bankers do this, and call it 'forward guidance'. For example, when the Bank of England issues forward guidance on interest rates (which is really a fancy name for telling people what it believes will happen in the economy, and how it will respond) people can make investments with more certainty, which in turn helps to create the calm conditions in which those forecasts have a better chance of coming true. The same applies to the people working in a business: if you can make accurate forecasts of trading conditions and the impact of your strategy, it means you can be more confident about long-term planning. This gives you the confidence to share those plans with the business, and this, in turn, helps your employees make better, quicker and more consistent tactical decisions, which are more likely to make your forecasts come true. This is a virtuous circle if it works well, but the essential component is that your initial forecasts must be well enough researched to inspire confidence in others.

If they are, they can help to focus staff: strong guidance that a particular market or customer will be a source of 352% growth, for example, helps to create a self-fulfilling prophecy.

Of course, there's the risk of being wrong. That's why in forecasting the reporting and understanding of errors and uncertainty is vital, which is what we turn to next.

15

WHAT COULD POSSIBLY
GO WRONG?

Holding a premortem will help you to forecast what could go wrong, as well as right.

Doug Hirschhorn, a coach who trains financial traders, says that even people who take risks all day, every day, fail to do this basic analysis. In interviews, he offers traders a hypothetical gamble that pays off 95% of the time. Would they take it? Out of twenty, nineteen immediately say yes. The twentieth insightfully asks, 'What happens if the gamble fails?'

'People don't care about fixing things when it's working,' he says, 'they care about how they are going to get paid.'

You've probably had this experience: the best point in a project is immediately after the first discussion. You've set out your goals, outlined the idea, maybe sketched out the way you will make your big hairy audacious goal into reality. You have an idea of the timescale and the resources you will need.

It's a little bit exciting, perhaps. You talk to your colleagues about how you can make it work.

You do some fieldwork. You find data on the size of the market, you get quotes from suppliers. You estimate the number of hours it will take. You make a big spreadsheet with all the good numbers. You make a presentation with all the numbers on it, and a special slide at the end that shows how much money you will save, or how many customers you will win over.

This might all be valid, but it's only half the story: it's a narrative, not an analysis. To create an accurate assessment, you need to investigate the chances of something going wrong, and the impact this would have. This is often very hard to do when you are making a plan, because the focus of your project is its success. No one wants to be a buzzkill.

The psychologist Gary Klein has created a technique to improve the quality of the analysis that he calls a 'premortem':

'If a project goes poorly, there will be a lessons-learned session that looks at what went wrong and why the project failed – like a medical postmortem. Why don't we do that up front? Before a project starts, we should say, "We're looking in a crystal ball, and this project has failed; it's a fiasco. Now, everybody, take two minutes and write down all the reasons why you think the project failed."'

Without a premortem, our optimism bias means we focus on collecting data on the causes and effects of success. The premortem, Klein explains, creates an incentive to come up with similar data on the causes and effects of failure.

Daniel Kahneman, again: 'My guess is that, in general, doing a premortem on a plan that is about to be adopted won't cause it to be abandoned. But it will probably be tweaked in ways that everybody will recognize as beneficial. So the premortem is a low-cost, high-payoff kind of thing.'

The challenge of coming up with hard numbers on both sides of the debate remains. Both success and failure are counter-factual: they are imagined futures, and often we don't collect good data on failure.

A premortem will throw up several possible bad scenarios to add to the spreadsheet. It's often hard to find failure numbers, so improving the effectiveness of your risk analysis might mean finding data in your own business, for example, on budget overruns, or failure to meet deadlines. Your project might be the exception to these everyday failures but, in a premortem, treat it as if it is the rule.

The second is to model the risk and cost of these problems as objectively as possible – for example, by asking someone outside the project to do it. You will end up with a range of possible outcomes: a good project plan lists the probability of different problems, and the range of impacts of those prob-lems. Your premortem may decide that you have a 50% chance of making £100,000 and a 20% chance of breaking even – but also uncover a 20% chance of losing £100,000, and a 10% chance of losing £500,000 (of course, this is massively simpli-fied). In this case, we add up the averages, and expect to lose money on the project (the expected return = 0.5 x 100,000 + 0.2 x 0 - 0.2 x 100,000 - 0.1 x 500,000 = a loss of £20,000). If, however, you adjusted the project – maybe by insuring it – so the big loss was capped at £200,000, your expected payoff would be a profit of £20,000 minus the cost of that insurance.

Whether you attach numbers to the forecasts or not, premortems are creative and effective ways to improve forecasting, because they provoke discussion and research into a full range of risks and rewards, not just a few emotionally preferred options. In the words of Doug Hirschhorn, they stop us thinking only about 'how we are going to get paid'.

WHAT'S THE WORST THAT CAN HAPPEN?

You can't eliminate risk, but unless you quantify it, the fear of the unknown stops you taking good decisions, as well as bad ones.

Modelling the risk of your decisions is extremely complex. But any decision that requires a forecast (which is most of them) has some level of uncertainty, and therefore implies that you evaluate the risk of doing it. If you don't, you're not making decisions, you're hoping for the best.

A lot of the day-to-day risk models we use are not sufficiently sophisticated. This is partly because sophisticated models quickly become extremely complex 'black boxes' that no one understands. Black boxes tend to create their own special brand of risk management: people input numbers, and if the computer says yes, we do it. This is what caused the 2008 financial crisis. Just saying.

So the best way to manage risk is to produce a model – a simplified version of the effects of a decision that makes logical sense – and then treat it with scepticism. We make models all the time in our spreadsheets but, when we use them for prediction, we tend to be overly deterministic. If sales projections are for 4% uplift, we multiply last year's number by 1.04 and use that as the input to calculate the profit.

At the very least, there has to be a range. If you bother to read your pension forecast, you will find that there are three scenarios: high growth, average growth, and low growth. It doesn't take long to produce these three scenarios on the spreadsheet.

By this stage, you should also have decided what your risk appetite is. Some business units don't chase high returns, because the cost of failure is high – regulated industries, safety-critical businesses or simply customer service for example. On the other hand, some areas have extremely high returns for winners that invite risk-taking. What the economist Joseph Schumpeter called the 'creative destruction' exemplified by technology companies is in this category. This defines an unacceptable level of risk and helps set clear (and responsible) incentives.

Using your acceptable risk level, you can attempt some form of expected return calculation on the spot (we'll deal with more sophisticated returns calculations next). This is extremely basic, but the results are sometimes surprising.

The expected return is always the sum of all the possible returns, multiplied by the probability of achieving that return. So the expected score from rolling one die is:

$(1/6 \times 1) + (1/6 \times 2) + \ldots + (1/6 \times 6) = 1/6 \times 21 = 3.5$

Take the probability of the low return, as a decimal. If it's 40%, that's 0.4. Multiply it by the amount of the low return (which might be a loss, a negative figure). Do the same for the other scenarios. Add them together. If the number is negative, on balance, you can expect to make a loss and you've got a strong argument that you should not even be considering taking that decision.

This is a simple rule of thumb exercise, but use this as a way to quantify the output of emotional forecasting processes, alongside the premortem.

The idea known as black swan theory, popularized by Nassim Nicholas Taleb, needs your attention. There may be a small chance of a disastrous result. This rarely gets modelled seriously, but why not? The problem with risk is that it isn't linear. The consequences of big success (suddenly you need more investment, and you won't be able to support your users) can be as bad as the consequences of extreme failure. It's tough to do this sort of analysis on a spreadsheet, but if you model the consequences of extreme events it might help create a contingency plan, or make you decide to spend money on insurance.

As well as being nonlinear, risk is dynamic. It changes due to events outside your control (e.g. weather, competitors) and as a consequence of your actions. What you do in one area of your business also increases risk in other areas. Again, these are complex situations to model, so it might be better to schedule a recalculation of your risk once a month. A survey-based way of doing this would be to ask everyone involved to evaluate whether the risk of an event was higher, lower or about the same as last time. This avoids groupthink. It also means you can quantify the changes in risk profile: three quarters think that option A is more risky, but only a third think option B is more risky.

Finally, avoid the temptation to extrapolate forecasts as a straight line, years into the future. Modelling risk is about undermining false confidence, as well as giving us reassurance that we're making the best decision possible. But, if you've ever bet on a sure thing or written down what you'll be doing in five years, you know the power of the confidence illusion.

17

IS IT WORTH IT?

The most important forecast of all: the return on investment.

Return on investment (RoI) calculations are everywhere, but they are subject to all the problems, caveats, false precision and biases of other forecasts. They are, however, a necessary evil. If you don't know what the return on an investment is likely to be, you don't know whether to make it, make a different investment, or just sit on the cash.

There's not a single method for determining the future value of an investment, but all of them start with a clear calculation of the effects that the investment would have on the business, and the value of that difference in cash terms.

So the return on investment of a new computer application over three years could be determined by estimating how much time it would save, and multiplying that by the wages of the people who provide the labour; how much additional business it would make possible; how much it would save on licensing compared to the old application, and so on. Subtract the cost of buying and maintaining it, and you get a number. It's clearly going to be a range rather than a single number: you might want to express most likely, optimistic and pessimistic values.

Another way to think of this calculation is to work out the moment at which your investment will have paid for itself: this is the 'payback period', usually expressed in months.

Alert readers will be saying: 'But surely business conditions might change over the payback period?' Very true. That's why calculating a range of possible returns is important, especially in a fast-changing sector like information technology.

Whatever the payback period, you might have to make some investments anyway: think of the return as being the difference in the money you make if you didn't make the investment. In some cases, (such as connecting your branch office to the Internet) your income if you don't make the investment will be more or less zero, so the decision makes itself.

When a return of the investment isn't inevitable, or there's a decision to be made between two options – for example, should you open an office in region X or region Y? – one of the most common methods that you will see to estimate the quality of the investment is called Net Present Value or NPV.

NPV estimates the lifetime value of an investment by adding and subtracting all the cash flows related to it, each year, for the duration of the investment. So if the investment makes a positive contribution of £5 million in year two, £10 million in year three and so on, you add these together make a total return. But first, you discount the value of the contribution in future years – for example, if your discount rate is 10% per year, you multiply the £5 million by 0.9, and the £10 million by 0.92, and so on, just like compound interest. Why? Because a return two years from now is less valuable to you than having that cash in your hand today. The choice of the discount rate is important: it is a measure of your impatience. It also expresses uncertainty: if your market is volatile, you discount the projected future returns more, because they are less likely to actually happen.

If you subtract the initial investment cost from this figure, the outcome may be positive (in which case this investment would be a better use of money than not doing anything). If it's negative, you'll be richer if you just keep the money in the bank. Financially, a project with the best NPV among all the forecasts you make would be the one to choose.

There's no need to get bogged down in the detail of these calculations (this is what accountants and finance directors do), but being able to read a document that contains them is an important skill. It's also an important way to think about forecasting. Often a forecast isn't so much about whether a project or investment is a good idea (there are many good ideas), but whether it is a better idea than the next best alternative, or whether it's a good idea 80% of the time, an okay idea 19% of the time, or a total disaster 1% of the time. Or, a forecast might establish that we simply don't know enough about the future to make an informed judgement more than a year ahead. In which case, don't just pick the middle number and cross your fingers. A wide range of projected returns means that you'll need to re-run these numbers regularly when conditions change, as they always do. Forecasting returns will be a business process rather than a one-off project.

PART 5

ARGUING USING FACTS

THE RAW AND THE COOKED

Just because the data tells a story doesn't mean the story is always true.

The elegant phrase 'raw data' is misleading. Data is usually cooked, for good reasons. Knowing how to cook it, and knowing when the cooking has been done well, is vital if you're going to win any arguments using data. And, if you're trying to change things, you're going to have an argument here and there.

Also, knowing about the cooking process is important because there's almost certainly going to be someone in your future who will try to use science stuff that isn't true to make a fool of you.

Understand how your own data is cooked

The most obvious way in which your data will be cooked is that you can't measure everything, and so someone has decided what you do measure. Because only things that are measured get reported, and because only things that are in the report are likely to be managed, this seemingly obvious problem has profound consequences. We see it in the way companies budget, for example: the way budgets are constructed helps to decide what we give money to.

Some of the unmeasured unknowns are also ignored because they are hard to measure. It's harder to measure how happy people are, than how much money they spend. So we don't manage happiness as well as we manage money. (We assume that people who are richer are happier. Not true. This works until you get to an income of about $70,000, after which, re-search shows, we don't report greater satisfaction with our lives as we get richer.)

Some of the unmeasured data is unquantified because it's just too hard to do it. The numbers are out there somewhere, but it's hard to put them together. Financial numbers are often hard to add up in detail, because they are assembled from many reports. Risk analysis is hard because risks change, some are extreme events with huge consequences, risks are inter-linked, and we can't predict everything that everyone will do.

Keeping numbers in silos is a way to cook data. The most dra-matic example was the spectacular bankruptcy, in 2002, of WorldCom, a company with $30 billion in annual revenues, which wasn't so much cooking the data as cooking the books. Auditors later discovered that its balance sheet had been overstated by $75 billion, and its income overstated by $11 billion. How was this possible? The major reason was that it ran many different accounting systems that didn't share data.

Double counting was common.

The most common problem throughout is that people feel they own particular data, and so don't share it. Even though you, hopefully, don't work in a company like WorldCom, your arguments may be compromised because you don't have the full picture.

Understand where other people have cooked the data

People tend to fix the facts (sometimes on purpose, sometimes accidentally) and skew conclusions. Some of this is incompetence, some is malice. Here are three ways data can be badly cooked before it is served to you:

- Selective evidence. In a 2013 study, a researcher called John Ioannidis from Stanford University picked 50 foods from a cookbook at random, and found that 80% of them had at least one research paper that showed they caused cancer as well as one that showed they prevented it. But a beetroot salesperson will only show evidence for one side of the story.

- Bad causation. A famous research study showed that smoking made it more likely you would commit suicide. Horror! Years later it was debunked when researchers also demonstrated that smokers were twice as likely to be murdered. Clue: the causation runs the other way. Depressed, stressed or imperilled people were more likely to smoke.

- A weird time frame. The start and end year might matter. If someone tells you that growth has been 5% a year since 2007, what would it have been since 2006, or 2004? Often the time frame is cherry-picked by checking which year gives the best result. Has global warming been occurring in recent years? The shape of the graph depends on what you call 'recent'.

How do we deal with cooked data? The most basic lesson is to be extremely sceptical of who is telling you the thing they want you to believe. The associations found in what statisticians call 'voodoo polls' that get reported in national newspapers, then instantly forgotten, often have as much to do with who is paying the bills as what happens in the real world.

The second lesson is to be extremely suspicious of one-off results. Surprising results get more attention, but that doesn't mean they are truer. If we find a link in data again and again, that's a good indicator that there's something to see. If we see the result sometimes and not others when we repeat the experiment, then the method is to blame. Numbers don't lie, but when we cook them they can sometimes fib a bit.

HOW THE SAUSAGE WAS MADE

Research data is always biased in some way. What matters is not trusting bad evidence too much.

Here's an interesting graph that a company called C Space uses to convince us that its services are good value:

Outperforming the market

Here's how our clients have grown compared to the Standard and Poor's 500 index. The correlation is simple. Partner with your customers and your business will be more profitable. (What does this graph mean?)

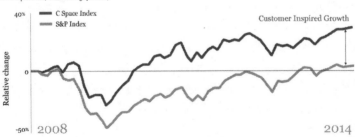

That's impressive, we think, the difference between the grey and the black lines is the value that C Space creates. Note that their explanation is more conservative: 'partner with your customers' is the difference, not C Space.

But the evidence for that is pretty flimsy too.

When you want to use statistics to make a comparison between two samples, or to learn about an entire population (for example, all of your customers) from a sample (the ones for whom you have data because they answered a survey), by far the most important thing is to know that you are comparing like with like.

So, if you have a survey of 200 of your customers, is that a representative sample? You hear about this often when political opinion polls hit the news after an election because their predictions were inaccurate. It's very hard to find a sample of 1,000 adults that 'look' like the entire electorate. They would have to be from all over the country, have the same range of qualifications, incomes, likes and dislikes as the whole population. There are all sorts of problems that might occur. For example:

- Often polls are done on the internet. But poor people and old people use the internet less, and so your sample will be too rich and too young.

- Sometimes people can 'vote' voluntarily in a poll. In which case the people who have the strongest opinions are more likely to be included.

- Sometimes people tell you what they think you want to hear, and then go and do something different.

- Some people seek out incentives – for example, being entered in a prize draw. They don't spend much time giving considered answers, because they are only there for the prize.

Now look again at the graph. What's wrong with that? We can't conclude much unless the companies in each sample are the same, except for the fact that they used C Space. It might be a part of the story, but here are some alternative stories, which may (or may not) be true:

- Companies that make large profits outperform the stock market. They also have more money to spend on external consultants, and so more profitable companies, on average, might be in the C Space Index.

- Maybe C Space targets successful companies to do business with them, because those companies pay their bills faster.

- Maybe a particular type of company tends to do business with C Space, and that type of company is in favour with investors at the moment.

This is also extremely important when you're looking at your own data. It's common for marketing departments to put out email surveys: 'Please tell us what you think…' Companies like Survey Monkey make it easy to produce good-looking surveys, and you probably get two or three a week. Let's imagine that you sent out a survey asking chief executives, carefully selected from your mailing list, what they think of your company, and whether they intend to spend more on your products in the future. When you get the replies, you find that 72% think you're doing a great job, and 67% will spend more in future.

Let's use our logic on this result:

- How many successful chief executives that you know have the time to do email surveys? Your replies may contain a high number of underperforming CEOs, or a large number of CEOs who ask their PAs to reply to non-urgent emails like this.

- Imagine that most CEOs are mildly dissatisfied with you, or can't quite remember what you do. They won't bother to return the survey – but this would be important information if you had it.

- Did you suggest (even accidentally) that there would be a reward for 'good' answers, for example a discount, or more customer service? You'll get more replies from respondents who want the reward and may tell you what you want to hear.

So you can't take a big gamble on this type of evidence. But you can use it as a suggestion to help narrow down choices, or as an indicative response that might suggest more research is needed. Cheap sausages look much the same as posh sausages, and graphs and pie charts that are made with biased data look just as convincing as those made with good data. As with the sausage, what matters is what went into making the graph, not what it looks like.

20

CORRELATION IS NOT CAUSATION

Data can't usually tell you why, only what.

You've probably heard this before, but might be vague about what it means. Here's the executive summary: if someone says there's no smoke without fire, they're wrong.

Correlation between two things means that if we see one happening more often, we also see a change in how often we see the other one. Causation is stronger: but when two variable quantities move together, we assume that one is causing the other – we may not be right.

These three things are examples of correlations: your body mass index (BMI) and your chance of a heart attack; the number of tweets about a TV programme and the number of people who watch it; per capita cheese consumption and the number of people who die by becoming tangled up in their bedsheets.

But which ones are causal relationships? It's vital we know about this because decision-making is a process of pulling imaginary levers. If we pull a lever, we want to know what is likely to happen as a result, and we are often given terrible advice by people who mistake correlation for causation.

So, let's deal with these situations in reverse order. The last one is, on the face of it, preposterous. It's one of the examples created by Tyler Vigen in his very entertaining web site Spurious Correlations, which has many more examples of things that appear to move together by a fluke. This is an effect of the availability of data nowadays. We measure thousands of trends and so, by chance, unrelated variables will go up and down at the same time. We avoid this by creating a hypothesis to test before looking at correlations, which we deal with later in the book.

Spurious correlations are why you can simply collect a big pile of data and reach into it to pull out linkages. You'll find few important causal relationships – but an unknown number of nonsense correlations too. Businesses distract themselves all the time with this process. In this instance you are unlikely to assume causation, but what if the relationship was more plausible?

The statistic about tweets and TV audiences is more complicated. There may be a causal relationship here, but there are at least three causal scenarios:

- Social works: when people tweet about a TV programme, it encourages people to watch it

- TV gossip: when more people watch a TV programme, they like to tweet about it

- Inspired by quality: good TV programmes have high audiences, and provoke debate

This really matters if you work for a TV company. What do you use social media for? It is tempting to believe the first scenario: invest in encouraging people to tweet, and your audience goes up. Many companies have used similar justifications to decide their social media budget, and discovered that nothing happens when they artificially stimulate the number of tweets. Maybe the causation is the other way round: you tweet about what you do. In which case social media is still useful, but it's an informal audit of what your customers are doing instead.

Scenario three might also be true though, which means that the best way to spend money isn't on social media, it's on a better script and decent actors.

Three scenarios may all create the same correlations: A causes B, B causes A, or C (unmeasured) causes both A and B. Working out which is which is a discipline called econometrics. If we have enough data, we can look for two things: do we see the effect when A happens before B, but not when B happens before A (in which case we might guess that A causes B); and, holding all other things constant (e.g. quality) does A still cause B?

Evidence accumulates over time and through a number of observations, and so we can say with some confidence that BMI is related to heart disease. We know this because we can be sure that having a heart attack does not raise your BMI, so B does not cause A. We can still see the effect when other variables (genetics, job stress, etc.) are constant. And we see the relationship through time, and in many locations.

You won't have the time, money or enough data to establish causal relationships about everything you see in your business. But there are two informal tests you can do:

- The smell test: If someone tells you that A causes B, can they give a convincing explanation as to why it should be true? If no one can come up with a convincing narrative, then there's probably another factor at work.

- The replication test: Even something that passes the smell test might be a fluke. So, once you have spotted the relationship, do you see it again the next month, or in another office, or with other customers?

Some causal relationships are interesting, but not important. When you've established that A causes B, this might not be useful because you can't change the thing that drives the effect. Giving a job to your best staff means it's likely to finish on schedule, but you can't improve your reliability by giving them more work, because they're already busy. You need to find another causal relationship that you can affect: better recruiting, investing in training or allocating work more intelligently.

It's surprisingly difficult to differentiate correlation and causation in practice, but you don't need the skills of an econometrician to makes better decisions. Apply your two tests, and then work out if there's anything you can do. And, if you've eaten a lot of cheese, be careful not to get tangled up when you go to bed tonight.*

* Not really

21

TOO MUCH INFORMATION

When there's a lot of data, how do we avoid paralysis by analysis?

In the mid-noughties Netflix decided to award a $1 million prize to anyone who could improve the company's recommendation algorithm by 10%. It inspired data scientists all over the world to set to work. After three years, the prize was won on 21 September 2009, by a team called BellKor's Pragmatic Chaos.

How did they do it? To quote from the paper published by team member Yehuda Koren: 'On the Restricted Boltzmann Machines (RBM) front, we use a new RBM model with superior accuracy by conditioning the visible units…'

On second thoughts, let's discuss why this was such a difficult problem instead. The challenge: because it offers thousands of films and TV shows, it is difficult for Netflix to suggest which one you would like best. If you shop at Amazon or similar sites, you will be accustomed to useful hints – 'Customers who bought this item also bought'. For Netflix, this is too unreliable if you're picking a way to spend your entire evening. When you log in to Netflix, it wants to suggest the perfect movie for you, based only on what it knows – which is mostly what you've watched before, how you rated it, how often you choose particular types of film, and a few general details about the world, such as your location and the time of day.

The science bit

This doesn't seem like a particularly difficult problem, until you try to solve it, and realize there are billions of different combinations of these variables. Netflix isn't unusual. Most real-world decisions that we make are similar: at work, you're asked to change something, you're often set a target to reach when you make the change. Though, unlike Netflix, you're not usually offered $1 million if you improve by 10%. We examined correlation, the property of two variables that we use to make predictions. When we say that 'the more we see of this, the more we will see of that', in the simplest interpretation we are saying that:

$y = a + bx$

This is the equation of a sloped straight line. We can measure (or observe) x, multiply it by b, add a, and use it to predict y (forecasters might also take the logarithm of x, or square x, or do all sorts of other tricks, but that's getting complicated). The slope of a best fit line through all the data points (recall this from Part 2) shows how much you need to increase x by to get an increase in y. So, in 2010, the British government used this method to calculate that every 1% increase in the duty on cigarettes (x) would raise an additional £25m in tax (y).

In the real world, we never, ever see such a precise relationship. So, when we are using facts to make predictions, the equation is more like this, where we measure lots of different influences on y, but can't measure all of them:

$$y = a + b_1x_1 + b_2x_2 + ... + error$$

In this case 'error' doesn't mean you made a mistake, it's just a way to lump together all the other things that might affect y that you haven't measured, and ignore them. You want this error to be as small as possible, but there's a trade-off here, because we usually want to say 'if we do a little bit of this one thing, what will happen?' In the government's calculations, we can ignore the other influences for a 1% change in duty, but you probably wouldn't make £250 million in tax by raising duty by 10%, because it would make people more likely to cut down, to give up, to start to buy all their tobacco duty free, and so on. We've boiled the decision down to the likely effect of one thing on one other thing.

Should I go to the pub?

If I wanted to predict the quality of my night in a pub, there are again many variables. I'd think 'who else will be there?' or 'do I like the pub?' In reality it would also depend on the weather, my day at work, the state of my bank account, how far I have to travel, and so on.

And yet, we humans magically make decisions all the time without drawing graphs. We often successfully manage to pick a movie we like without the help of a computer. In real life we perform an imperfect version of the $y = a + bx$, based on heuristics (mental shortcuts) that are quick but sometimes wrong: for example, we watch a bad movie or have a dull night out and wish we'd done something else. 'It seemed like a good idea at the time', we think, 'ah well, lesson learned.' The heuristic was a bad argument. We learned from experience, and have adapted the heuristic for next time.

In business, relying on heuristics means you argue for more things because they seem like a good idea, rather than by arguing from evidence. But the alternative may be paralysis by analysis. So how can we train ourselves to make good decisions, without having to get a qualification in econometrics?

1. When it's a sure thing, do it. The 'sure-thing principle' is simple, but rarely followed. Often in meetings we get hung up because we don't have information that, while interesting, wouldn't change our decision. So, if you're wondering whether to hire Bill to design your web page, someone might ask you to hang on for a week, because Emma might become available, and you can discuss it then. Stop! If Emma were available today, would you still hire Bill? If the answer's yes, make the decision now.

2. A weaker version of this principle can help you decide. Is the cost of getting the information you need (in time, inconvenience, maybe paying for data) bigger than the likely value of that information in improving your decision? If it is, don't bother. The Netflix prize is an example. Incredibly advanced though the winners were, their improvements were never implemented. Why? Because the additional accuracy did not justify the engineering effort that would have been required.

3. Eliminate options by comparison. You have five options.

Don't try to compare them all, compare them in pairs, based on a defined set of criteria. If A beats B, you don't need to compare B to C, because all that matters for the decision is how C and A compare.

4. If you're only sure of one thing, change that, and wait until you know more to do other things. This isn't a foolproof way to get to the best possible result, but it's a way to use data to make progress. If you're faced with a big project with many moving parts, and you know from your data that, if you change nothing else, making one change to one of those moving parts is a good decision, do that now, and analyse one other moving part next month. This is the foundation of 'agile' methodologies, which we cover in more detail in the next section.

Learning how to compile and analyse data is only half the battle. Learning how to use the data to clarify debates, rather than complicate them, is a complementary skill that's possibly even more valuable.

22

MR RIGHT, OR MR RIGHT NOW?

The best data can sometimes be worse than no data at all.

Every decision relies on timing as well as correctness. For example: pricing. Food retailers launch around 8,000 new products in the UK every year. Think about it: that's 30 new products every day. The difference between success and failure can be a simple matter of a few pence on the price.

But we often find out about failure when it's too late to do anything. You can find out that a promotion has failed for sure three months later, when it is interesting but useless information. It might be better to know with less certainty after three weeks, or even three days.

We've gone into great detail about what might make survey data unreliable: small samples, biased samples, opt-in surveys, and measurement errors. All of these can be corrected or reduced with time and care, but this precision might be pointless.

What do you do when right now is more important than right? The most important point is not to slow yourself down by collecting too much data: for example, you might not need to know why one thing is better, or how much people prefer it, when the answer to the simple question: 'Do you prefer A or B?' is all you need to know. So asking one or two questions, or finding out one thing, often can be enough to make a decision.

Here are some techniques:

- The informed gut-check: an email survey to a small group can pick up a sense of where you are in a lunchtime. Send out an email asking people to score one thing on a scale of 1 to 5, and they're more likely to let you know than if you ask them 10 questions.

- An SMS survey: two questions max, gets an immediate answer.

- Ask them at the right time. A machine on the till with two buttons. Was your product easy to find? A single 'question of the day' on the website will catch people when they're in the moment – so you get small data, but research shows it's often more honest because our memory of an experience is often unreliable.

- Check social. Want to see what people are saying on Twitter? It's not the whole truth, but it might show that most people haven't even noticed your crisis (or that they think it's funny).

- Research by walking around: if you want to know what people in the office think, go and ask them now by walking over to their desk and writing down their response. Hey, millennials, don't worry: back in the old days we used to do this all the time.

Of course, over-surveying is the danger here, and that's why it's best to make these quick surveys as lightweight as possible. They're limited, but being able to make an argument in real time using limited data is just as valuable as being able to research a 60-page report.

PART 6

THE DATA-DRIVEN MANAGER

23

COPYING ISN'T MANAGING

History may be written by the winners, but don't let them write your business plan too.

David McRaney, a consultant who specializes in this sort of cognitive bias, says, 'The advice business is a monopoly run by survivors.' But why is that a problem? They earned the right, after all.

Rule one of being a data-driven manager is to trust your own information, because it's the most complete data you'll get. It's a lot more complete than the advice we're routinely given by, well, everyone.

If you are one of the 400 million people who uses LinkedIn, you might well get a regular email full of advice from success- ful people, who basically tell you how to do things the way they do things.

It's not just LinkedIn, of course. Business magazines and books are stuffed full of advice from successful people, and most of it seems to make sense while you're reading it. But if you listen to enough advice, you will be advised to do absolutely everything at the same time. At Amazon, CEO Jeff Bezos says that asking people what they need is the key to innovation: 'we start with the customer and we work backward.' Meanwhile Steve Jobs, the other great technology entrepreneur of the last 10 years, held the opposite opinion: 'people don't know what they want until you show it to them.'

In the words of the Dire Straits song: 'Two men say they're Jesus, one of them must be wrong.' The best you can say about these two pieces of advice is that they're both ways to make decisions, so possibly both are better than doing nothing. But how can you know what's right for you?

In my latest email from LinkedIn, Arianna Huffington, founder of the *Huffington Post* tells me that I should join the 'sleep revolution'. Jack Welch, who built GE, advises me to 'love micromanaging'. Someone called Brian de Haaff ('Brian seeks business and wilderness adventure'), who is an entrepreneur, claims that customer success teams make salespeople obsolete. Professor Bill George of Harvard Business School says I should 'put down the phone' if I want to be more successful.

This all seems very entertaining, in as much as I'm going to ignore all of it. But 'life lessons' from successful people are addictive. Surely, this is data: if you want to succeed, the best way to succeed is to consult as many people who have succeeded in the past, and find out what they did. It's inspiring, it's interesting, it's practical, and it is statistically extremely dangerous.

That's because, statistically, we shouldn't just listen to winners. We can divide success into two parts: success that was the inevitable result of careful planning and analysis, and which nothing could derail. We'll call that 'perfect success', because it doesn't exist. Then there's success that is a combination of planning, timing and some other features that we will bundle together as 'luck'. Luck is something good that you couldn't foresee. By definition, you can't plan to be lucky.

So, if you're planning to launch a restaurant, the fact that Ohio State University found that 60% fail in three years and 80% fail in five years is very useful to know: because you need to collect data from the full sample, not just the one in five that were the winners. Or worse, only the ones that blog on LinkedIn.

If you look at the full sample, you can understand luck better. You can plan to minimize the chances of an unlucky failure. When we see success, we often rationalize what happened – we make it into 'perfect success' in our minds, and then maybe try to copy every little bit of it. But some proportion of the losers would have done the same things, been just as professional or innovative, and still not succeeded. Maybe it's failure that you should be examining, not success.

In his book *Thinking, Fast and Slow*, Daniel Kahneman points out that 'A stupid decision that works out well becomes a brilliant decision in hindsight... If you group successes together and look for what makes them similar, the only real answer will be luck.'

INTUITION OR DATA?

The answer is both. You can't do business on instinct alone, but you probably can't do business without it either. The trick is to know when to employ it.

Before we bury ourselves too far in data, we need a reality check: while many business decisions could benefit from more data, few benefit from using data and nothing else. As one of the twentieth century's greatest economists, Arthur Pigou, once asked: 'Who would ever think of employing an economist to run a brewery?'

Instinct is a useful decision-making tool for survival that has developed over thousands of years. The important thing in business is to use it when it gives you the best information you can get, meaning you have time to do analysis when that's better.

Analysis takes time and effort. In 2000 the business writer Neil

McAllister invented a fictional comic strip superhero called Action Item who flies in, spouts office jargon and flies out again. 'We need you to put a stop to Dr Diabolical's nefarious plan', says the panicky police commissioner. 'To fully own the challenge I'll need to be goal-oriented and results driven!' the superhero replies, pointing out that is 'far too early to drill down… this is just a high-level meeting.'

We all know Action Items, those whose ability to plan careful analysis is matched only by their total uselessness in a difficult situation. To avoid becoming Action Items we all use the mental shortcuts known as heuristics every day, simply to function: we can't think through every tiny decision, because there would be no time left to act. So instinct is a way to avoid over-thinking when it's not useful. You might have heard this described as 'System 1' thinking: automatic, involuntary, and almost effortless. Good System 1 thinking is especially useful in a crisis, when Dr Diabolicals have nefarious plans for us.

Much of the early research into decision-making concentrated on how to put structures in place for making decisions, on the biases and limitations of System 1, and how not to be fooled by instinctive thinking. In the 1980s the psychologist Gary Klein and his colleagues realized that this wasn't always a useful way to think about real life – for example for soldiers, firefighters, nuclear power plant operators and emergency room doctors, too much structure is as bad as none at all. Making the correct decision too late in a crisis has results that are as bad as making the wrong decision.

Klein and his colleagues created a framework called 'naturalistic decision making', which seeks to harness the good aspects of intuitive thinking: accepting that we make many decisions in ways that we can't easily explain, the framework explores how to make System 1 work optimally. The trick is knowing the limits of your gut, and when to trust it.

He's not without his critics (Daniel Kahneman, the other giant of research into decision-making, is one of them). But even Klein's harshest critics accept that intuition isn't always bad, even if it is just a starting point that helps us to discard useless information.

Keen readers will have spotted that this is a circular argument: if you ignore information, how do you know it would have been useless?

Klein and Kahneman frame the problem of trusting your gut differently: perhaps Klein is 'glass half full', Kahneman 'glass half empty'. They have occasionally collaborated to try to find common ground. They still don't agree, but we can generalize some basic rules. So when do you trust your gut, and when do you use data to be a better manager?

Time is always a factor. Data is useless if you can't get it before you need to make a decision. Research into chess grand masters shows that they can quickly identify a situation because they have learned hundreds of thousands of situations, and can quickly match the board they see to the contents of their mental filing cabinet. Even if the rest of us could perform the same analysis, it would take impossibly long.

Relevant data isn't always available. Sometimes we simply can't know enough, and so have to apply knowledge from other situations instead. For example, you're a doctor. The patient is unconscious and alone. You can't wait for him or her to come round to ask more questions, so your thinking is framed by your experience of similar patients that you or your colleagues have treated in the past (on the other hand, any relevant data is better than none at all: fire-fighters learn what's inside a burning building before they decide whether to run into it).

To rely on data, the situation must be the broadly the same today as when you collected the data. The point about the examples above is that the situations, though difficult, are known, so the risk of a surprise is minimized. Chess has rules; the human body doesn't spontaneously develop weird new diseases, except in horror films. But business constantly throws up novel problems caused by many factors, some of which are unknown unknowns.

So you are forced to rely on instinct when you need to decide right now, or if you can't find out any more useful information. But beware: in every situation, thinking without data is made riskier by our own biases, and limited knowledge of the context. Kahneman would argue that instinctive decision-making is far more flawed than we perceive.

In reality, it isn't an either/or situation. You will always use bits of both – if data was all we needed, then all the best companies in the world would be run exclusively by data scientists and accountants. For example, Gavin Patterson, the CEO of BT Group, says that instinct is something he actively looks for in a senior manager; but a company that is building infrastructure that costs billions of pounds, with a payback of 10–20 years, isn't going to be able to start a project on a hunch.

25

WHAT IF?

You test staff. You test products. Why not test decisions too?

Hal Varian wrote two of the standard economics text books that have tortured students through the years, but lately has also been employed as the chief economist at Google. You can understand why Google might want accountants to add up all the cash it's making and minimize its tax bill, but what does it need an economist to do?

In short: experiments. Varian's textbooks are about economics as something abstracted, a set of mathematical models. In a world of Big Data, he says, the really valuable economists are the ones who can translate this into something you do.

Experiments are one of the most important ways in which Google learns what to do next. 'You all know about big data. But big data can often only show association, not causal relationships. To learn in Google, at any point in time, we are running some 1000 experiments,' Varian says.

Earlier I explained why correlation is not causation, and that there are ways to judge whether one thing is likely to have caused another thing. The best way to do this, if it is available to you, is what is called a randomized controlled trial. You pick two groups, call them A and B, at random to perform the experiment. You change only one thing for group B, and see if the members of group B get a different result. If they do, then the thing you changed has most likely caused the result to be different.

You'll be surprised to know that Google has probably experimented on you. For example, it is constantly changing the way it orders search results to try to get the most useful things at the top of the list. To see whether a change works, it might use the new way for half of the people who search, and the old way for the others, and see which one is more useful to us.

Big tech companies have an advantage when doing this, because they have millions of customers every day. They can randomly give us two different layouts of a web page to see which one generates more sales, or even test a new typeface or logo.

You might not have that luxury, but you can approximate it (with caution). The world is full of 'natural' experiments, which are situations in which just one thing changes. Every decision you make is a natural experiment. Measure the situation before your decision (for example, the number of sick days that your colleagues take). Measure the number after. Compare the two carefully, using comparable numbers. Build this discipline into your projects (often we're so delighted just to have made a decision, and so fearful that it wasn't the right one, that we don't revisit it afterwards).

The problem is that the data might mislead you. Most natural experiments are a flawed basis for decision-making. Here are some examples:

- In San Francisco, research conducted by the Municipal Transport Authority reported the number of monthly rides per taxicab declined from 1,424 per month in March 2012 to 504 in July 2014: a 65% decline, which it blamed on the arrival of Uber. The problem with this experiment: you would expect to get a different result in these two samples, because taxis in San Francisco are much less used in July, and the number of taxis on the road had increased. Other data didn't support the conclusion that Uber was bad for the taxi business. When a taxi firm did an analysis from October 2012 to October 2014, it found that fares per taxi had gone up by 3%.

- Graduates in 2010 earned on average £16.10 an hour in the UK, but those who just finished school and then got a job earned only £10 an hour. Therefore, a degree is worth £6.10 an hour for every hour you work in the future, right? Wrong. The samples are different: the people who got a degree would probably have earned more anyway, because they had better results from school, were most interested in high-paying jobs which needed a degree, and so on. So the difference is due to many factors, not just one.

- In Germany, introducing better rights for fathers who wanted to take paternity leave meant that six times as many fathers took time off to be with their babies, so would this be the effect of shared parental leave in the UK? Again, highly unlikely. In Germany, for example, job security is higher. So you cannot apply what happened in one experiment to a different population.

On the other hand, you experiment with products, so why not test decisions? To do this:

1. Measure the initial conditions carefully, and measure other factors so you can measure unintended consequences (for example, you might sell more but have to work more hours). Careful measurement of initial conditions is essential.

2. Think about testing a decision by having two groups, the control (no change) and the treatment (change), so you can measure the difference. But also try to make the groups as similar as is practical, and be careful that you're not seen as punishing one group – for example, by randomly restricting lunch breaks.

3. Watch out for seasonal or local effects. Summer and winter, town and country, online and offline are different and will yield different results.

4. Are you testing your decision on the same people who will use it? An example: testing something only on junior staff, then applying it to managers, is not a good test. Testing on your staff and then applying it to customers is also clearly problematic.

5. Be prepared for no. For example, if you test a new email system by giving it to half your staff, and their efficiency drops and stays lower than the other half, have a strategy to roll it back.

6. Be prepared for yes. A simple experiment may be to pilot a change, or test two suppliers. If the pilot works, you need

to leave enough time and budget to agree a change and implement it.

Two final warnings: not all differences in outcome are meaningful. Some results that look like success may just be random: you won the experimental lottery. This is hard to discover, and needs some statistical training. A simpler way to get a better idea of whether it was a fluke: repeat the experiment with a different test group. Also, even if the result isn't random, the size of the effect might not be important. Recently a market researcher told me that he found a way to use Twitter activity as a way to forecast future sales. It was, he told me, 60% as reliable as counting the activity on the company's webpage. But you can already count the activity on your webpage for little or no cost. The experiment was a success, but a completely pointless one.

26

THE LIMITS OF CERTAINTY

In risky or uncertain situations, don't jump to conclusions

Imagine you're going to hospital to be tested for a disease. The test is 99% accurate, and 99% of the population is disease-free. Or, to put it another way, there's a 1% chance you have the disease, and there's a 1% chance of a medical error when you take the test.

The doctor walks into the room and says: 'I have bad news. You tested positive.' What is the likelihood that this is wrong?

You're probably thinking that it's 1%, or 1% of 1%. Not so! In this situation, this diagnosis would be wrong half the time. Half of the people who tested positive for the disease would be disease-free.

Think about that for the moment: if you got bad news from this imaginary hospital, you wouldn't actually know if you had the disease or not with certainty better than a coin flip.

If this has temporarily blown your mind, and you don't understand why, let me draw you a table. Across the top, the situation (disease or no disease) and down the side, the test result (positive or negative). Imagine the doctors test 10,000 people. The first column is the people who walk in to the hospital with no disease: that's going to be 9,900 people (99% of 10,000). Of those 9,900 people, 1% will be unlucky enough to get a false positive test due to medical error. So that's 99 false positives, who are told by the doctors that they have the disease when this isn't true.

	No disease	Disease
Positive test	99	
Negative test	9,801	
	9,900	100

Now let's fill in the column for the people who have the disease. Of the 100 people who have the disease, 99 will have it correctly diagnosed, and 1 will get an incorrect diagnosis (a false negative).

	No disease	Disease
Positive test	**99**	**99**
Negative test	9,801	1
	9,900	100

Read across the top line, in bold, to find out who gets told they tested positive. In this situation, if you get bad news, it's a coin flip whether it's true or not – and in real life, medical tests aren't 99% accurate.

This doesn't just apply in medicine. We often use outcomes to modify our prior beliefs without justification. This is an aspect of what's known as Bayesian statistics, which is the foundation of much of artificial intelligence. First formulated by the Reverend Thomas Bayes, who was one of those eighteenth century vicars who used his spare time to be a genius at something else, it is becoming increasingly influential because it gives us a toolkit for using big data.

Our limited application, in this case, is a simple insight into conditional probability: The chance of B, given A is not the same as the chance of A, given B.

We often confuse the two: the chance that someone who is a drug addict is unemployed (high) is not the same as the chance that someone who is unemployed is a drug addict (low). In our example, the chance that someone who gets a positive result is sick (half) is not the same as the chance that someone who is sick gets a positive result (99%).

Uncertainty in initial conditions, even when we can estimate it with accuracy, can often mislead us if we base our decisions only on outcomes.

A business example: let's call it the blame game. You devise a set of tests to recruit the best staff. Based on your track record, you're 90% sure you can identify the right people. And you also know that you've got a great chance of success: market conditions mean that 10% of your projects will fail with good staff. With bad staff, they will all fail.

You put your staff on to this new project, but it's not a success. Imagine we ran this experiment 100 times. This is the result we would expect to see:

	Good staff	Bad staff
Fail	**9**	**10**
Succeed	81	0
	90	10

So, when you're doing the post-mortem on the failure, what should you blame, your bad choice or bad luck? You probably want to blame bad luck, but it's marginally more likely that you accidentally picked bad staff.

So, should we trust hospital results, and should we toss a coin to find out who is to blame for business failure? No need. The best way to become more certain would be to repeat the process, this time only on the people who failed. In the hospital example, you would be invited for further tests if you tested positive the first time (or, simpler, have more than one test on the day). Repeating our medical test on the people who tested positive the first time would result in only one false positive instead of 99, and one further false negative (write the table again, starting with 99 people in each column, if you're wondering why).

Similarly, giving your team a second chance may be good management. In risky or uncertain environments, a one-off result often doesn't mean what you think it means.

27

SPEND MONEY WHERE
IT WORKS BEST

Budgeting is often anchored in what you spent last year. But the past is often not the best guide to the future.

Why do companies budget? Because budgets help them control costs and make people accountable for the money they spend. But, while having no budget control and lots of people spending money is clearly a route to disaster, how that budget is calculated isn't as obvious as it seems.

Throughout this book there's a theme that, to make data work inside a business (or a family, or even in your own life), you have to be able to use facts to challenge the status quo. John Maynard Keynes is supposed to have said that when the facts changed, he changed his opinion. 'What do you do?' he asked his inquisitor. The answer for most of us is that we tend to hang on to old ideas for too long, in the face of the evidence.

Many business processes are set up so that they protect the status quo. People will often accept a sure thing, or have an exaggerated opinion of the value of what's happening now. Or, if you prefer things to rhyme, remember Hilaire Belloc's ironic cautionary verse: 'Always keep a-hold of nurse / For fear of finding something worse.'

In 1970, Peter Pyhrr published 'Zero-base budgeting' (ZBB) in the *Harvard Business Review*. His argument was that, if you want to create a budget that will be optimal for the year ahead, the year just gone is not necessarily the best place to start. Instead, budgeting should break down the company's activities one-by-one, evaluate how much they cost and what the return is, and then prioritize spending based on that. The results are often very different from the outcome of budgets that are adjusted from previous years.

ZBB became a cool idea for a short time, but went out of fashion: not least because it was very hard to do. Recently, McKinsey has reported it is back in vogue: in 2015, 90 companies mentioned it in their communication with investors (only 13 had two years earlier). It seems to have made a return because in the last 10 years many companies have been running out of ways to sustain growth, and so need to look again at what they do. The easier availability of numbers that they can use to make the calculation helps.

You can do a ZBB exercise as a table-top exercise, or within a business unit (you can do it for your department, or even your own family if you like, it's the same principle). Separate each activity, and the money spent on each part of it. Then work out what each activity is contributing, and how to best spend the money to get the same, or better, results. Don't let the person who holds the budget do this alone – have someone prepared to challenge ideas and ask awkward questions.

The result might be a fundamental re-evaluation of the business you're in, because some cherished activities don't seem to be contributing much, or have become cash leaks for benefits that no one can quite remember.

When's the best time to do this? McKinsey works with many private equity companies, whose reason for existing is to buy failing businesses and reorganize them to make them more efficient, so it finds many of them are open to this type of exercise. But understandably, you might not want to wait to be bought, or for failure, to think about this. In general, the right time is a time when the burden of proof in the budgeting process changes from 'Do we need to change this?' to 'Why are we doing this?'

What tools do you need? Data is embedded in this process at every level.

You must be able to break down your costs into small units. Not easy, this bit. Some costs go across business units, for example services that you share (an office building is one). But others do not, and you need to be able to estimate the cost of cutting back, or cutting off.

You must set targets. Reallocation of priorities has to be done in the service of something, and the consequences of cutting costs might be different to the consequences of setting higher growth goals, or trying to focus on fewer types of activity, or simply having more fun without going out of business.

You might need to change how you measure the business. The existing budget structure has probably given rise to a number of ways to behave, not least the trackers that measure how well you're doing based against a fixed investment.

Most importantly, you need to trust the process. And so we come back to this, yet again. ZBB is a process that is based on hard facts. Existing budgeting processes mix intuition (this must be a good thing to do, because we're already doing it) with a smattering of data-driven decisions (we will make small adjustments). How successful you are may be an indicator of how much you trust the numbers that you measure. If people don't trust the data, it might be because they are not accustomed to working that way. Or it might be because you need better numbers.

ZBB seems like a crazy idea to people who have been used to traditional budget setting. And for exceptionally stable, carefully managed businesses, basing next year's budget on last year's might be the lowest-cost way to do the process, if not the outcome that's most efficient. But often businesses take this route not because the situation is stable, but because the cognitive bias known as 'anchoring' convinces them that the best thing is the thing that they do already, even in the face of all the evidence.

To make a ZBB project fly, data on how budgeting can be improved is (ironically) not always the best way to convince, because you have to get rid of this cognitive anchor. Imaginative exercises, for example asking if you were assigning advertising money to each project, how much would you give to each, can start to tap into people's unconscious valuation of projects. Or: if you were starting the company today, and we had to rank our excitement about the potential of each unit, what would that ranking be? ZBB is still a minority activity, but it's cheap to test for a small project, and at the very least it may help to measure risk and return in new data-driven ways.

28

KNOW YOUR POTENTIAL CUSTOMER

Is selling to your best customers driven by data or relationships? Both – but data increasingly comes first.

CSC, a giant American technology and services company, thought it knew its biggest customers well. But when it did some research into their buying process, CSC discovered that, on average, about 30 people contributed to the process, and that even its best salespeople knew about only a small fraction of them. As a result, it created a programme to research the others, finding their contact details, their interests, their responsibilities, and where they fitted in the procurement process.

What we know affects the options we consider, not just the quality of those decisions. One of the most powerful examples is the focus inside B2B sales teams on product profitability. That's how most companies sell, but it's not how their customers buy.

We value what we measure. Sales teams tend to measure the profit of the things their company does or the things the company makes, not their value to the customer. But when McKinsey surveyed 200 business customers, their biggest complaint was a lack of knowledge among the people who sold to them, while at the same time 55% said they were contacted too frequently.

What else can you do? The technique known as account-based marketing (ABM) argues that conventional sales (start with a product, work out what you believe its key advantages are, market those features and benefits, and then go to your customers and ask them if they have the same needs), gets this all backwards.

Instead, start with a key account you want to sell to, and collect better data. Who, inside that business, influences a sales decision at the earliest stage? What would that person respond to? What do you know about their problems? When will they be starting the next round of decision-making?

This is a data-driven operation. At its simplest, you need to collect the names and details of all the people who influence a sale. Not all of them will influence it in the same way, so you need to know what they need, and how it's best to contact them. This data is used to market to them only the things they need: it might be education, it might be a meeting, and it might be an audit of what they are doing now.

ABM uses data to put both right: have a limited number of high-value interventions, with the correct people at the right time.

Clearly you can't do this for everyone and be profitable. You must also have some data that qualifies your key accounts as key: it may be growth potential, or the sophistication of their need, or that your share of their business is small. The last one is the toughest but potentially most valuable – if your sales team has poor relationships and they have resisted your marketing so far, it's tempting to write them off. ABM suggests that maybe you don't know enough about them.

Will it work for you? It doesn't work for everyone. For a start, it replaces a sales push with a business development plan, and creates marketing that is tailored not only to single customers, but also maybe to individuals inside that customer. It takes at least six months to collect the data and use it to make a difference, warns marketing specialist ITSMA.

On the other hand, data from those who use it implies that better information provides better results. The 2014 ITSMA member survey suggests that 84% of marketers who measure RoI describe ABM as delivering higher returns than other marketing approaches – of whom 42% say it delivers significantly higher returns.

Much of this book is about finding numbers and statistics. This is a different type of data, but it should fit seamlessly into the projects listed above. Indeed, it increases their meaning because it gives the numbers some context. For example, a dashboard that tracks client engagement could also capture tweets by target contacts, or news about key accounts. The central principle is the same: when you have deep information, you can make quick, effective management decisions.

29

IT NEVER ENDS

Be inspired by agile programming techniques to continuously use feedback to improve.

Throughout this book, I've constantly reminded you that data is only useful if it can be used to change your decisions. The well-worn quote about the misuse of facts (attributed to A. E. Housman, David Ogilvy, and others) is that 'many use statistics as a drunken man a lamp post: more for support than for illumination.'

While a decision made with the backing of evidence is better than a decision made purely because you believe it to be correct, in practice it's a moot point if the same decisions get made. As we have seen, guessing has two advantages that data often doesn't have: guessing is cheap, and it's quick.

So, the best result would be building data analysis into a process of creativity that can be used to quickly and regularly improve what you do. That's the foundation of what are called 'agile' development methods, which were created for software development in 1986, and are now often used for other design processes.

We can best define the agile approach by what it isn't. Usually we define a project at the outset, marking stages along the way, using our best customer or market data to define what success looks like. As the project progresses through its milestones, it may succeed on its own terms, but ultimately fail: when it is delivered it may, for example, turn out that what customers want has changed, or that what customers thought they wanted wasn't what they really needed. In software, this process ensured that 83% of projects failed.

Agile methodologies break the project into smaller 'chunks', which are worked on by small groups, delivered in days rather than months. At each stage the prototype is evaluated, with daily updates and weekly reviews: this can be for efficiency (how quick is it to do something), or effectiveness (do people find it easy to find information? do they like it?). That information is constantly used to plan the next stage, or re-evaluate decisions or goals. Management is bottom-up and feedback-driven, rather than top-down and ideological.

You can see how it works with software. But agile approaches are increasingly used in other activities. A natural way to use agile methods is for website design, but you can use it to test new processes, or forms, or even internally to check how staff respond to more efficient ways to run your business.

Here's an example: Bruce Feiler, the author of *The Secrets of Happy Families* thinks that more families can be run in an agile way. So, instead of the parents setting external and timeless rules for bringing up the kids, the individual chunks are made into accountable checklists. He learned this from research with a family called the Starrs, where the four children adopted the agile methods that their father used at work. Feiler now uses this at home with his own kids: 'We ask three questions: what worked well in our family this week, what didn't work well, and what will we agree to work on in the week ahead? Everyone throws out suggestions and then we pick two to focus on.'

This process extends to all sorts of unlikely areas. For example, he let his kids define their own punishments. They decide how to spend their allowances. The trick is that everything is measured against the standards set for them, and mistakes are corrected the next week.

How does this work in business? The trick is to have an engaged (and relevant) group of testers. Employees, managers and customers might rate the same idea differently, so make sure you're collecting feedback from the people who are most relevant. Follow this feedback: even if it results in a wrong turn, you can correct the course again the following week. And make the feedback clear and actionable: clear ratings are better than vague statements of approval. Finally, there has to be a clear goal and mission to work towards – it helps clarify the feedback process. If you are making a product that is easier to use, don't obsess on what colour it will be.

Agile methodology, driven by constant feedback, is a perfect example of building data-driven decisions into an area normally governed by rigidity or management by instinct. It is a difficult concept if you're used to gut-feel, top-down planning. But, if Feiler can use it to successfully manage his five-year-old twin daughters, using it in your work should be a piece of cake.

PART 7

WHY YOU NEED TO BE DATA-DRIVEN

30

SIX REASONS NOT TO TRUST YOUR GUT

Surveys show that 40% of major decisions are based on a manager's gut feel. But our intuition is often wrong. Data-driven decisions save us from ourselves.

Every time data is hard to find, or it shows your decisions in a bad light, or someone questions whether the data-driven you is really an improvement on what went before, you'll be tempted to close down the spreadsheets, delete the dashboards, and do it like you did before. So keep this chapter handy for those times.

If you copy any strategy because it seems like an appealing idea, you are basing your decision on instinct. When management consultants Accenture surveyed British, Irish and American businesses in 2010, it found that roughly two in five important business decisions were made this way.

If you play roulette for long enough, the house will win. If you ignore data and trust your gut for long enough, you might do well in the short run. But you're not likely to have a hot streak that's going to last your entire career, especially when you're up against the combined power of instinct plus data in your competitors.

So here are six reminders of why gut feel is flawed.

Gut feel ignores other people's needs

Just because you're comfortable with a decision doesn't mean it's the best idea for everyone else affected by it. For example, it's easier to be brave in an office than if you work on the shop floor and have to pacify angry customers. It doesn't mean that it's even the best decision for you when you're in a different mood.

Gut feel is about the past

Gut feel can be consistent, even when the world has changed. When all you have is a hammer, everything looks like a nail. A great example of this is the now almost-forgotten hero CEO of the 1980s and 1990s, 'Chainsaw' Al Dunlap. He got his name by pioneering the cult of downsizing: going into failing companies and firing underperforming staff and bad suppliers, then selling on the company a few years later. His antennae twitched when he spotted waste: cutting was the answer to every problem. But eventually he ended up in a giant company (Sunbeam Inc.) in 1996 for which cutting wasn't the answer, and in two years he drove it into the ground: even the day that the board fired him, he responded by announcing redundancies. Sure, he identified waste and got things done, but when he was put in charge of a company that wasn't very wasteful he missed the real problems: at Sunbeam they were poor quality and lack of innovation. He had no idea, because his gut hadn't been trained to spot those things.

Gut-feel success or luck?

Another problem with acting on instinct is that your brain might have made the wrong associations in the past. You made a decision, and you perceive that something good happened. But the decision or the action might not have been the cause. The effect might be an illusion, and couldn't be measured ('people were much happier after I did that' – how do you know?). The effect might have occurred, but by a random chance, like winning a lottery after going to church. We look for reasons and, if we're not careful, find the wrong ones.

Gut feel creates groupthink

If something feels right, it may be because the people around you feel good about it too. It's easier to trust instinct when there's no challenge. But that's how financial bubbles form: we all believe something to be true, and continue to invest in it against the weight of evidence.

Why do we do this? Partly because our psychological makeup stops us from listening to what the facts are telling us, and instead we listen to others. We tend to make the same mistakes (over optimism, impatience) at the same time.

Gut feel stops us learning

The wonderful opportunity of measuring, using data and recording what you do and what happens afterwards is that you can change your mind. The raw material of learning is new information. We want the best raw material possible. Your opinions, or those of other people, are poor quality materials.

We naturally assume everyone else is wrong

In a sample of more than 600 residents of the United States, more than 85% believed they were less biased than the average American. In 1977, a famous experiment found that 94% of professors rated themselves cleverer than their colleagues. Another experiment showed that 32% of the employees of a software company said they performed better than 19 out of 20 of their colleagues (think about it).

This is the number one gut feel bias: the illusion of superiority, which convinces us that we're the only person thinking clearly. Often the opposite is true. The worse we are at something, evidence shows, the more our self-image departs from observed reality. We have a bias blind spot.

When the psychologist Irene Scopelliti and her colleagues attempted to measure the bias blind spot experimentally in 2015, they found some worrying problems with it:

- It is consistent. On the one hand, this is good: it means we know it exists and can plan around it. On the other, you don't have a bias blind spot just because you're irritated, for example. It's there in the same way that the blind spot at the back of your eye is there.

- It is not linked to intelligence. You can't be too clever to have a bias blind spot (and not knowing you're biased doesn't make you stupid).

- It is not related to your decision-making ability. The size of your blind spot does not make you more or less decisive as a problem solver, even though it will affect the quality of your decision.

- It is not related to self-esteem. Egotistical people have the problem in the same degree as other people (though it may be more obvious).

This is a tricky problem at work. This bias affects our ability to take advice – if you've got a big blind spot, and so need advice the most, you're likely to be most resistant to taking it.

That's why data isn't just for the times you want to look at it, because the times you assume you don't need it are likely to be the times you need it most.

To be data-driven, you have to build it in to every relevant business process. One simple way to help reduce our blind spots is to have rules, formal or informal, which decide which decisions can be taken without data. In some regulated industries, of course, this is absolute: you can't launch a drug without testing it. But, for example, when the retailer Tesco introduced Clubcard, it suddenly found it had a goldmine of (often counterintuitive) information about its customers, and many managers who were certain that they knew best regardless of the numbers. In response, Tesco created a culture that, in meetings, the data had a voice: when something was discussed, it wasn't decided without looking at the figures first.

If we want to be 352% better, good data should always have a voice: we know it protects us from the bad decisions of other people, but we often don't fully realize that it's also protecting us from our own inner idiot.

RESOURCES AND FURTHER READING

Software that helps you become data-driven

There are hundreds of applications and vendors that will sell you software to capture data, organize it, format it and use it for analytics. I can't list them all, so I've stuck to a few that I've mentioned in the text. As ever, the reference doesn't mean I'm endorsing one vendor as better than any other.

DropBox is a centralized file store: http://dropbox.com

Google Drive centralizes your data too: https://www.google.com/drive/

Toggl will record the time you spend doing different tasks: https://toggl.com/

TweetDeck is Twitter's social media platform: https://tweetdeck.twitter.com/

Sprout Social has strong analytics: http://sproutsocial.com/

SocialOomph attempts to measure the impact of your social media: https://www.socialoomph.com/

Transcribe uses machine learning to offer low-cost transcription: http://bit.ly/DDtranscribe

Kaggle: a community of data scientists: https://www.kaggle.com/competitions

Research and resources

CIMA: 45% of SMEs don't use regular management accounts: http://bit.ly/DDaccounts

Atlassian: The time you waste at work, quantified: http://bit.ly/DDtimewaste

Open Data Institute: http://bit.ly/DDodi

UK Government data: http://bit.ly/DDdatagov

Edward Tufte and table design: http://bit.ly/DDtuftetable

Spurious Correlations: http://bit.ly/DDspurious

The Netflix prize: http://bit.ly/DDnetflixprize

Action Item comic strip: http://bit.ly/DDactionitem

Naturalistic Decision Making: http://bit.ly/DDndm

The anchoring bias: http://bit.ly/DDanchoring

Agile TED talk by Bruce Feiler: http://bit.ly/DDagile

Net Promoter System blog: http://bit.ly/DDnps

IPA resources on social media measurement: http://bit.ly/DDmeasure

The trouble with tracking, by Jan Hofmeyr: http://bit.ly/1UoSxIP

When can you trust your gut? Kahneman and Klein in conversation: http://bit.ly/1UoSTz8

The Economist: Why don't more people learn from failure?: http://bit.ly/DDfailure

Bloomberg: How Survivorship bias tricks entrepreneurs: http://bit.ly/DDsurvivor

Forbes: Naomi Robbins demonstrates effective graphs: http://bit.ly/DDgraphs

Why dashboards fail, by expert Stephen Few: http://bit.ly/DDdashboard

McKinsey: The return of zero-based budgeting: http://bit.ly/DDzerobase

An account-based marketing blog: http://bit.ly/DDabm

Books and journal articles

Cole, K.C. *The Universe and the Teacup: Mathematics of Truth and Beauty*. United Kingdom: Abacus, 1999. If you think you can't enjoy numbers, this book will show you another world – as it says, of truth and beauty.

Gitelman, Lisa, ed. *'Raw Data' Is an Oxymoron*. Cambridge, MA: MIT Press, 2013. If you're interested in how data is cooked, this has a lot of detail.

Huff, Darrell. *How to Lie with Statistics*. New York: Norton, W. W. & Company, 1993. The first and best book about how the presentation of data can mislead you.

Kahneman, Daniel. *Thinking, Fast and Slow*. London: Penguin Group, 2012. Interesting and easy to read, the explanation of System 1 instinctive, heuristic thinking, and its uses.

Kahneman, Daniel and Gary Klein. 'Conditions for Intuitive Expertise: A Failure to Disagree'. *American Psychologist* 64, no. 6, 2009: 515–26. The two experts on System 1 and System 2 thinking worked together to create a paper on when to trust your gut, and when not. Text here: http://bit.ly/DDdisagree

Mayer-Schönberger, Viktor and Kenneth Cukier. *Big Data: A Revolution That Will Transform How We Live, Work, and Think*. Boston Eamon Dolan/Houghton Mifflin Harcourt, 2013. This book explains the basics of big data, and what it can do, without jargon. Read the first chapter for free: http://bit.ly/DDbigdata

Mecklin, John M. 'The Tyranny of the Average Man'. *International Journal of Ethics* 28 (2), January 1918: 240–52. What do averages obscure? This 100-year old paper started the debate. Read it here: http://bit.ly/DDtyranny.

Paulos, John Allen. *Innumeracy*. New York: Vintage Books, 1990. A mathematician explains how we get big and small numbers wrong, how we don't understand risk or chance, and what we should all do about it.

Reichheld, Frederick F. and Rob Markey. *The Ultimate Question 2.0 (Revised and Expanded Edition): How Net Promoter Companies Thrive in a Customer-Driven World*. Boston, MA: Harvard Business Review Press, 2011. Net Promoter Score and its uses explained by the creators of the system.

Singh, Simon. *The Simpsons and Their Mathematical Secrets*. United Kingdom: Bloomsbury Publishing, 2013. It probably

won't help you to manage data, but the mathematical jokes hidden in The Simpsons will give you a reason to watch the re-runs.

Varian, Hal R. 'Beyond Big Data'. *Business Economics* 49 (1), 2014: 27–31. Google's chief economist explains how the company uses experiments.